MW00535368

TAROT FOR CREATIVITY

Tarot for Creativity

A Guide for Igniting Your Creative Practice

By Chelsey Pippin Mizzi

With illustrations from the Modern Way Tarot

CHRONICLE BOOKS

SAN FRANCISCO

FOR MY FIRST TAROT COMPANIONS:

Kat Dunn, who started it all;
Pamela Colman Smith, whose artful
illustrations have made all the difference;
Rachel Pollack, without whose books
I would be lost.

Text copyright © 2024 by Chelsey Pippin Mizzi.
Tarot card illustration copyright © 2024 by The Modern Way Tarot.

All rights reserved. No part of this book may be reproduced in any form
without written permission from the publisher.

Library of Congress Cataloging-in-Publication Data available

ISBN 978-1-7972-2555-5

Manufactured in China.

MIX
Paper | Supporting
responsible forestry
FSC™ C169962

Design by Kayla Ferriera.
Border illustrations by Henna Crowner.

10 9 8 7 6 5 4 3 2 1

Chronicle books and gifts are available at special quantity discounts to corporations, professional
associations, literacy programs, and other organizations. For details and discount information, please
contact our premiums department at corporatesales@chroniclebooks.com or at 1-800-759-0190.

Chronicle Books LLC
680 Second Street
San Francisco, California 94107
www.chroniclebooks.com

Contents

Introduction *A Mirror and a Map* ◆ 9

How to Use This Book ◆ 13

Tarot 101 ◆ 17

Part I: Your Creative Heroes
THE MAJOR ARCANA ✳ 22

Take Creative Risks with **THE FOOL**	24	Check Your Privileges and Margins with **JUSTICE**	57
Manifest Your Ideas with **THE MAGICIAN**	27	Surrender Control with the **HANGED ONE**	60
Find Creative Depth with **THE HIGH PRIESTESS**	30	Kill Your Darlings with **DEATH**	63
Cultivate Your Creative Environment with **THE EMPRESS**	33	Avoid Creative Burnout with **TEMPERANCE**	66
Build a Creative Structure with **THE EMPEROR**	36	Stop Self-Sabotage with **THE DEVIL**	69
Seek Out Creative Mentors with **THE HIEROPHANT**	39	Embrace the Worst-Case Scenario with **THE TOWER**	72
Commit to Your Creativity with **THE LOVERS**	42	Reclaim Creative Self-Care with **THE STAR**	75
Compose and Trust Yourself with **THE CHARIOT**	45	Embrace Your Creative Phases with **THE MOON**	78
Do Hard Things with **STRENGTH**	48	Believe Your Own Hype with **THE SUN**	81
Follow Your Creative Vision with **THE HERMIT**	51	Rediscover Your Creative Roots with **JUDGMENT**	84
Navigate the Unexpected with the **WHEEL OF FORTUNE**	54	Make a Fresh Start with **THE WORLD**	87

Part II: Your Creative Toolbox

The Cups

Introduction to the Cups 94

Master Creative Abundance with the **ACE OF CUPS** 95

Deepen Your Creative Connections with the **TWO OF CUPS** 98

Celebrate Your Creative Achievements with the **THREE OF CUPS** 101

Reframe Creative Block with the **FOUR OF CUPS** 104

Navigate Rejection with the **FIVE OF CUPS** 107

Rediscover Creative Joy with the **SIX OF CUPS** 110

Embrace Your Potential with the **SEVEN OF CUPS** 113

Move On Meaningfully with the **EIGHT OF CUPS** 116

Take Pride in Your Creative Work with the **NINE OF CUPS** 119

Find Creative Paradise with the **TEN OF CUPS** 122

Get Playful with the **PAGE OF CUPS** 125

Connect to Your Creative Core with the **KNIGHT OF CUPS** 128

Be Your Own Safe Harbor with the **KING OF CUPS** 131

Cherish Your Creations with the **QUEEN OF CUPS** 134

The Swords

Introduction to the Swords 138

Cut Through Negativity with the **ACE OF SWORDS** 139

Uncomplicate Your Overwhelm with the **TWO OF SWORDS** 142

Let It All Out with the **THREE OF SWORDS** 145

Give Yourself Mental Space with the **FOUR OF SWORDS** 148

Challenge Your Ego with the **FIVE OF SWORDS** 151

Make Peace with Your Past with the **SIX OF SWORDS** 154

Confront Your Assumptions with the **SEVEN OF SWORDS** 157

Set Your Creativity Free with the **EIGHT OF SWORDS** 160

Acknowledge Your Anxieties with the **NINE OF SWORDS** 163

Quit Catastrophizing with the **TEN OF SWORDS** 166

Practice Beginner's Mindset with the **PAGE OF SWORDS** 169

Just Go for It with the **KNIGHT OF SWORDS** 172

Assert Creative Authority with the **KING OF SWORDS** 175

Rise Above Your Fears with the **QUEEN OF SWORDS** 178

The Wands

Introduction to the Wands 182

Find Your Creative Spark with the **ACE OF WANDS** 183

Use Your Imagination with the **TWO OF WANDS** 186

See the Big Picture with the **THREE OF WANDS** 189

Know Where You Belong with the **FOUR OF WANDS** 192

Brainstorm Effectively with the **FIVE OF WANDS** 195

Create Like You've Already Won with the **SIX OF WANDS** 198

Defend Yourself from Distraction with the **SEVEN OF WANDS** 201

Start and Finish Strong with the **EIGHT OF WANDS** 204

Navigate Creative Competition and Envy with the **NINE OF WANDS** 207

Don't Lose Sight of Your Vision with the **TEN OF WANDS** 210

Reclaim Your Attention with the **PAGE OF WANDS** 213

Have a Creative Fling with the **KNIGHT OF WANDS** 216

Keep Your Spark Alive with the **KING OF WANDS** 219

Take Up Space with the **QUEEN OF WANDS** 222

The Pentacles

Introduction to the Pentacles 226

Nurture Your Creative Gifts with the **ACE OF PENTACLES** 227

Balance Your Priorities with the **TWO OF PENTACLES** 230

Create in Community with the **THREE OF PENTACLES** 233

Respect Your Limits with the **FOUR OF PENTACLES** 236

Hold Space for the Hard Stuff with the **FIVE OF PENTACLES** 239

Give and Accept Creative Support with the **SIX OF PENTACLES** 242

Pause and Reflect with the **SEVEN OF PENTACLES** 245

Hone Your Craft with the **EIGHT OF PENTACLES** 248

Invest in Yourself with the **NINE OF PENTACLES** 251

Appreciate Every Creative Day with the **TEN OF PENTACLES** 254

Embrace Ambition with the **PAGE OF PENTACLES** 257

Trust Your Creative Worth with the **KNIGHT OF PENTACLES** 260

Ground Yourself with the **KING OF PENTACLES** 263

Come Home to Your Creativity with the **QUEEN OF PENTACLES** 266

APPENDIX I: Sample Reading for Creativity ◆ 270

APPENDIX II: Journaling with Tarot ◆ 273

APPENDIX III: Tarot Spreads for Creativity ◆ 276

Acknowledgments ◆ 287

About the Author and Artwork ◆ 288

A Mirror and a Map

Creative block is the *worst*.

You know the feeling—when you sit down in front of a canvas or a screen, even when you open your mouth to say something clever or thoughtful and your brain goes dry as a bone. You wonder if you've ever had an original or worthy idea in your entire life. And. It. Feels. Awful.

But creative block is also a fact of creative life.

And make no mistake: We all live creative lives.

You may be an artist, a writer, an entrepreneur, a teacher, a manager, a consultant, a content creator, a coder. Whatever you do, your work and lifestyle rely on creative thinking. On new ideas. On problem solving.

But new ideas, especially *good* ideas, are tricky beasts.

Sometimes they have to be pried out like teeth. Sometimes they flutter around in your brain like butterflies, impossible to pin down. The process of finding them, or catching them, can be so exhausting that you're worn out before you can even begin to take action.

I get that. As a writer, coach, and entrepreneur, I feel that overcoming block and overwhelm

is a daily challenge for me, too. I need to have ideas, and enough energy to execute them, across all of these identities. And I have to free myself from expectations, including my own. I also need to take care of myself and keep my personal creative well full so I can live my life outside of my creative career.

I'm pretty good at it—good enough to help other creatives overcome creative block, overwhelm, and burnout to tell their stories, action their goals, and nurture their creativity through my coaching business. My clients have called our work together "the perfect balm for creative block," and said that working with me has helped them "gain clarity professionally, creatively, and psychologically."

But I didn't always have the stamina to show up in the world as my full creative self, let alone the confidence to help others empower *them*selves.

A few years ago, I was deep in the midst of an identity crisis. I'd been laid off from my job as a journalist, I'd lost the plot on yet another novel I'd invested years of time and money into writing, I couldn't confidently market a crowd-funding project I'd started, and I was stuck in a toxic vacuum of comparing myself to other more "successful" writers. I certainly didn't see myself as someone capable of making several bold career changes in the short span of two years, or the kind of person who could start her own business.

Creative block had consumed me. The pressure to make things, to tell stories—once the most magical part of my life—felt like an albatross around my neck.

Then, I found tarot. And slowly but surely, I got the magic back.

* * *

When my friend, novelist Kat Dunn, asked if she could practice reading the tarot for me, I was initially a less-than-enthusiastic guinea pig. I didn't want my future to be dictated to me—my past experiences with divination had felt disempowering and anxiety-inducing. I was sure, as a spiritual skeptic and all-around agnostic, that tarot wasn't for me.

Kat assured me future-gazing or fortune-telling was only one facet of the cards, one I wasn't required to engage with if it didn't work for me. She taught me that tarot can function similar to another meaning-making system that I was already intimately acquainted with: therapy.

A tarot reading, like a therapy session, is an opportunity to reflect and to plan—though tarot should be seen as a supplement to, and not a replacement for, a therapeutic relationship with a mental health professional.

Today, I rely on a combination of therapy and tarot to hold a mirror up to myself and trace the topography of my world so I can plot a map to help me get through life. If that sounds familiar to you, it's because it doesn't just describe tarot and therapy; it describes the creative process, too.

When we make things, we explore, reflect, and push ourselves toward the version of life we want to live. And that's why the tarot is such a powerful tool for creatives. It's a reflection of our experiences, an atlas for our hopes and dreams, a compass to lead us out of the sticky mess of block and toward a deeper, more collaborative relationship with our creative impulses and talents.

* * *

The first question I ever asked the tarot was about my creative journey. I was in the early stages of a new project, but feeling stalled. So, after Kat convinced me to give the tarot a try, I asked for advice and ideas to free myself from the fear and discomfort I had around moving forward with the book I was writing.

When Kat flipped over the three cards I'd chosen from her deck, my relationship with my creativity changed forever. I could feel excitement start to tingle in my fingertips as we poured over Kat's collection of tarot books, debating how each card's symbolism and history tied into my situation, and how that could help me think differently about my blocks.

I bought my first tarot deck online that night. (Some people will tell you that it's bad luck to buy your own deck, but most modern tarot readers disagree; the tarot is accessible to everyone, and if you feel called to get yourself a deck, no superstition or gatekeeping practice should stop you.)

As I started to learn about the tarot, what struck me most was its ability to help me understand the narrative and purpose of my life and my work. To make sense of disparate, even conflicting ideas I had about who I was, what I was doing, and why. To offer new connecting links I'd never thought of before.

I came to understand that tarot doesn't have to be a fortune-telling tool, or even a strictly therapeutic tool. It can be a storytelling tool. An idea generation tool. A creativity tool.

It just made sense, like I'd found the missing key my creative life had been lacking all along.

I've always written from images. At age ten, I won a citywide writing contest inspired by a painting hung in the Fralin Museum of Art in Charlottesville, Virginia. I was spellbound by the way a painting could open the door into a story, could set light to a long fuse of ideas and give my imagination fuel to erupt. *The Bay Window*, an obscure work by the American Impressionist Carl Frederick Frieseke, planted the seed for the first short story I ever wrote, about the friendship between a homesick young maid and the cautiously optimistic butler who helps her reunite with her family. I've been turning to paintings and photographs for inspiration ever since.

The more I studied the tarot, the clearer it became that the cards could do for me exactly what paintings and photographs had done for years. But they could do even more: I could lay out a series of cards to craft unique stories and ask new questions. The tarot didn't simply give me seventy-eight new images for inspiration; it also gave me a system of rich, interlinking narrative tools that could help me understand myself and my work in new ways.

Beyond helping me to free up writers' block, tarot prompted me to reevaluate my creativity on a broader scale. Before tarot, I'd never considered myself an entrepreneur, or a facilitator, or a coach—even though I'd always felt a passion for going my own way, and for leading groups: I landed my first writing internship because I'd been a self-starter, experimenting with content online for fun, which got me noticed; in my high school and college days, I directed student plays; and as a features editor and PR writer, I've used my skills to help lots of different people tell their stories. But it wasn't until tarot helped me connect the dots and see myself as an all-around creative, not "just" a writer, that I gave myself license to be truly bold for the first time in my creative career.

That's the discovery, the unblocking, that led me to start my business and write this book.

✳ ✳ ✳

Since 2020, I've helped hundreds of creative people from all kinds of backgrounds find creative empowerment through tarot.

Turning to tarot helped my client, Terra,[1] a solo entrepreneur, define the brand pillars of her online yoga service and develop a method for creating social media marketing content that feels authentic to her heart-centered business.

The cards have helped Nadine, an illustrator and Etsy seller, re-prioritize her work–life balance so she can find moments of creative inspiration through playing with her son, and come back to her business refreshed.

Taylor, an author, came to me to workshop the second draft of her novel. The cards gave her permission to follow her gut and cut out a lackluster love-triangle plotline. Thanks to a tarot session, Taylor ended up crafting a compelling, career-focused subplot that allowed readers to connect more deeply with the novel's

---

1. All names have been changed to protect my clients' privacy.

backstory, so they could root not only for
Taylor's heroine to fall in love with the hero
but also to fall back in love with her own life.

I've seen acrobats use the cards to inspire
new choreography, collage artists develop new
motifs based off patterns and textures in the
cards, essayists uncover thematic links between
disparate ideas, teachers rethink the medium
of a tricky lesson, and actors find character
inspiration.

Tarot can help you, too. It can help you show
up to your creative work and your creative life.
It can help you to dream big. To launch that
crowdfunding project, write that screenplay,
put together that ambitious proposal, program,
or event. And for those times when you're not
sure what you want or what to do, the tarot can
help you navigate creative block by offering
you new ideas, and by reminding you to take
care of yourself and find joy. Tarot will even
challenge you to leave behind projects, mindsets, and relationships that don't serve you or
your creative life.

Over the course of this book, you'll learn
how to use the tarot for creativity—to understand how tarot can open up a direct line not
to spirits or the future or the mind and heart
of your love interests, but a direct line to *you*.
To that magic well of creativity that you have
inside of you, just waiting to nourish your
dreams and ambitions.

How to Use This Book

This book is designed to help you get in touch with your creativity, live a more creative life, experiment with different artistic media and modes of expression, generate ideas for individual creative projects, and reflect on the highs and lows of your relationship with creativity.

In the following pages, you'll find a breakdown of each of the seventy-eight cards in the tarot. For every card, you'll get a suggestion for how to understand the card in a creative context, a unique tarot spread aimed to help you deepen your tarot practice and integrate the card's message into your creative life, and creative prompts inspired by each card.

You can read this book cover to cover, to help you get a big-picture feel for what the tarot has to offer for your creative journey, or you can use it as a dictionary of sorts, turning to it every time you draw a card, or anytime you need help when it comes to a specific creative issue. It is designed to be both an introduction to tarot as a creative tool and a lasting reference you can turn to again and again over the course of your creative life. The spreads and prompts will ensure that even once you've mastered the meanings of each card, you will keep making new discoveries about your creative experience every time you return to this book, and every time you draw a tarot card.

You may notice a discrepancy between some of my card descriptions and the imagery used in this book. While the text adheres closely to the original Rider Waite-Smith designs, offering a foundational knowledge of tarot tradition, the book features illustrations from The Modern Way Tarot, a deck created by Jiri Bindels and illustrated by Neil Fernando. The Modern Way cards offer fresh, contemporary interpretations of Pamela Colman Smith's classic imagery, adding dimension and depth to my own insight. Take what resonates with you from both the text and the image, leave behind what doesn't work, and use your own creativity to imagine how the different elements of this book can enrich your relationship with the tarot, no matter which deck you personally choose to work with.

Let the Prompts Inspire and Challenge You

For each card in the tarot deck, I've supplied four "creative prompts." These are not assignments—they are ideas, opportunities, challenges to your creativity. Most of them should be doable at home with whatever resources you have on hand (though a few suggest field trips!). Every card also includes a journal prompt, so that there's always at least one exercise that requires nothing but pen, paper (or your Notes app), and an open mind.

These prompts cannot, by any means, cover the full spectrum of creative expression, but they should get your creative juices flowing and give you just a little taste of how many different ways the tarot can inspire your creative mind.

Think of every prompt (and everything offered in this book, for that matter) as a jumping-off point for your creativity. Trust your own judgment and give yourself permission to break the rules and respond however you want to any tarot card you draw.

Don't feel hemmed in by a medium. If a prompt suggests you use photography, but you'd prefer to explore the idea through song, or to respond to the card in a completely different way entirely, trust your gut and go with it. That said, don't be afraid to let the prompts challenge you—just because you don't identify as a painter doesn't mean you can't explore a prompt through paint. The more creative risks you're willing to take with the tarot as your guide, the more rewarding your tarot practice, and your creative practice, will be.

At the end of the day, these prompts are here to help you—to show you what's possible, and to help nudge you into action when you're feeling disconnected from your creativity. You won't be inspired by all of them, and that's OK. But when you trust that giving the prompts a go is an excellent exercise in and of itself, you might be surprised by how much you enjoy the process.

Use the Spreads When You Need Them

Each card also comes equipped with its very own tarot spread. A spread is a sequence of cards, each with a specific meaning attached, designed to help you find specific guidance on a topic.

The spreads in the entries for the individual cards are relatively simple (requiring no more than four cards) and are designed to help you reflect more deeply on each card's message, generate ideas, and take action in your creative life. These spreads are not intended to help you predict your future, but to design the kind of creative life you want.

Like the prompts, the spreads are not required—you don't have to do the individual card spread every time you draw a card or consult this book; the spreads are there for you if and when you need them.

If you'd like some guidance on how to read a spread, turn to Appendix I for a sample reading. And in Appendix III, you'll find seven additional spreads for creativity.

Keep a Tarot Journal

I highly recommend keeping a tarot journal for your journey through this book. It's the easiest way to get familiar with the cards and a straightforward method of interacting with your creativity in a low-pressure way, which makes it a great tool if you're hoping to connect meaningfully to your creativity for the first time.

You can structure your journal however you like. The easiest way to start is to pull a daily tarot card from your deck and spend at least a few minutes reflecting on the prompts for the card you've drawn. Your journaling ritual can be fancy, low maintenance, or anything in between—the important thing is that you make space to explore your creativity and to reflect on the card. The knowledge in this book will only support you creatively if you commit to trying things out, giving the cards the time and space to work with you.

For more advice on how to start and maintain a tarot journaling habit, see Appendix II.

Trust Your Own Creative Impulses

As you make your way through this book, you'll develop your own personal way of working with the cards in a creative context. Some of that will be based on the advice in these pages, but a lot of it will be based on spontaneous moments of inspiration that arise from inviting tarot into your creative practice.

So, break the rules or follow them. Ignore my advice or take it. Just make sure that whatever you choose to do with the cards in your hands and the knowledge in this book, you're allowing your imagination, curiosity, and creativity to lead the way. Trust that whatever way the cards inspire you is the right way to work with them.

And if you come up with an exciting new way to use the cards to generate creativity, I want to hear about it! Find me on Instagram (@pipcardstarot) or email me (pipcardstarot@gmail.com).

I'm Not Creative—Is This Book for Me?

Allow me to let you in on a little secret: Developing recipes, or even just finding appetizing ways of serving something from your favorite cookbook, is an act of creativity. Turning someone else's trash into something stylish is absolutely creative. Solving problems through troubleshooting code requires ingenuity and creativity in spades. And the research and enthusiasm you need to take the holiday of your dreams on a budget—that's creativity at its finest.

Our culture has grand ideas about what creativity looks like: flighty, tortured, untouchable, magical. We equate creativity with being a genius, with being special, with being gifted.

But the truth is it's impossible to be human and not be creative. Our thoughts and the connections we make, the way those thoughts and connections lead us to unique actions and lifestyles, that's all creative.

Creativity *isn't* special—it's a fact of life. And that's what makes the tarot such a powerful creative tool.

Like creativity, tarot is something that appears magical but really isn't that special, and I mean that in the best possible way.

Both creativity and the tarot are about making connections, about finding magic through observation and action; they're not about waiting to be sprinkled with pixie dust or to suddenly inherit supernatural powers.

So, if you are doubting whether this book is for you because you don't think you're creative, or because you're not into witchy stuff, don't worry—it is.

You don't need to be a career creative to be a creative person. You don't need to be a psychic to be a tarot reader. You don't need to have even the tiniest clue what you're doing. You only need to be a human being.

No matter who you are, no matter what kind of life you lead, creativity is for you.

The tarot is for you.

And this book is for you.

This book is for the hobbyist baker and the Michelin chef, the Paris gallerist and the corner-of-the-page sketcher, the bestselling author and the bedtime storyteller, the cutting-edge 3D artist and the web-design-dabbler, the foreign correspondent and the travel blogger, the interior designer and the Pinterest queen, the indie-film darling and the vlogger, the nail artist and the muralist, the viral sensation and the shower singer, the community theater star and the Hollywood darling.

Wherever you're at on your creative journey is a good place. The tarot offers a mirror that reflects that place in all its glory, and a map to help you chart new creative waters whenever you're ready.

Tarot 101

You don't need to be a tarot expert to use this book, but there are a few basics, like the origin of the cards and some essential vocabulary, which will help create a solid foundation for your relationship to the cards.

What you'll find in the following pages is a whistlestop tour of the most crucial tarot knowledge you'll need to make the most of this book.

Where Did the Tarot Come From?

Legend has it that tarot dates back to the ancient Egyptians, when an occult order hid the secrets of spiritual enlightenment in plain sight by coding their doctrine into a deck of playing cards.

There's no actual proof of that, but I love the story, and it just goes to show how powerfully tarot can spark our collective imagination.

Here's what we do know:

While cartomancy, the art of using playing cards for divination, very well might date back to the ancient Egyptians, the tarot, as a specific cartomancy system, most likely originated in the 1400s as a European parlor game.

French tarot and Italian tarocchi decks were, and still are, made of up seventy-eight cards, split into five parts: twenty-two fully illustrated "triumph" cards numbered 1–21, plus a kind of wild card referred to in French as "l'excuse," and four suits, each made up of fourteen cards. The suits in a tarot playing deck are pretty similar to modern fifty-two–card playing decks, except they have four court cards (Page or Valet, Knight, King, Queen) instead of three (Jack, Queen, King), bringing their number to fifty-six.

In the fifteenth century, a number of wealthy Italian families had their own tarocchi decks commissioned, complete with bespoke illustrations—the triumph cards in particular were richly detailed. One of those commissioned games, the Visconti-Sforza tarot, become a major influence on the imagery and interpretation of modern tarot decks, and the rich visual language of the illustrations provided the early sparks for using the seventy-eight–card game for interpretative, reflective, and divination purposes, rather than parlor play.

Whichever origin story you buy into, both the ancient Egyptian myth and the cards' medieval history point to a crucial common thread that makes the tarot a potent tool for uncovering stories, themes, and ideas: its robust, interconnected symbology.

The tarot is a visual language. The seventy-eight cards are in conversation with each other. Motifs from one card will show up in another, linking them in interesting, surprising, and sometimes subversive ways. The tarot also draws on a number of meaning-making systems from around the world, including astrology, Greek and Roman mythology, Judeo-Christian mysticism, numerology, and pagan symbology.

Just like when you evaluate a work of art, read a novel, or watch a film, context is king. Understanding the basic archetypes and symbolic references at play can enrich your experience with the tarot and lead to a deeper, more expansive experience with the cards.

But the beauty of reading tarot through a creative lens is that you also get to apply your own meaning to the cards, to take what speaks to you and leave whatever doesn't serve you at the door.

Tarot Terminology

This book will help you decipher the language of the tarot so that you can use it to connect with your creativity and generate ideas. But before we get into how to use the cards as creative tools, there's a few basic terms to cover so that you can quickly feel at home when using this book.

ARCHETYPE

An archetype is a broad, universally recognized theme or image that offers shorthand for understanding a complex, yet universally recognizable idea. Oliver Twist is an archetypal Underdog, for example. Dr. Watson is the Loyal Friend, the Layperson, the Voice of Reason.

In modern entertainment, reality shows often deal in archetypes—the Party Girl, the Troublemaker, the Prince Charming—recognizable thematic identities we can understand within a few short scenes that tell us what kind of story to expect.

Archetypes can easily be confused with stereotypes, but these are two different things. An archetype is a storytelling device; a stereotype is a prejudicial belief—it shuts story down. A stereotype diminishes a person or thing, while an archetype invites us to look closer and understand our relationship with what's being represented. Archetypes are the broad strokes of ideas that we, as creatives, then fill in with the details of our own experience, perspective, and ideas.

Think of an archetype as your raw material: Fitzgerald's Daisy, Shakespeare's Juliet, Zadie Smith's Clara Jones, and Sally Rooney's Maureen may all be waifish ingenues that appear to be defined by their male counterparts' desire, archetypally recognizable as Damsels in some kind of Distress. Their authors, however, have used the archetype as a starting point, going on to craft rich, complex, and surprising inner lives for each.

The cards in the tarot are archetypal images. They offer a representation of something familiar to us, then prompt us to investigate, explore, and create our own relationship or craft our own narrative from that image.

COURT CARDS

All four suits of the Minor Arcana end with a court: the Page, the Knight, the King, and the Queen. For some readers, these cards might represent real people in their lives, but I've stuck to using them as archetypes to stand in for major themes in each suit.

Traditionally, the court card hierarchy moves from Page to King, with the King being the pinnacle of the suit, but you'll notice that I've switched the King and the Queen in the hierarchy in this book. In part, I've made this choice to subvert the patriarchal structure of the court, but also because Kings tend to represent outward, or perceived, mastery of the qualities of their suit, while Queens represent inner wisdom, discovery, and confidence, and that to me is the ultimate goal of your journey through each suit.

INTUITIVE READING

Reading tarot intuitively means that you rely on your own impression of any given card, rather than memorized "meanings" for each card. In this book, I invite you to do a little of both, because I think the most creative ideas come from combining your own interpretation with the added context of the predetermined language of the tarot. The essays I've written around each card in this book offer a combination of insights on the card's established meanings and my own intuitive interpretation of the card in a creative context. Through the creative prompts accompanying each card, you're invited to engage with your own intuitive reading of the card.

MAJOR ARCANA

This is the name for the first twenty-two cards in the tarot, starting with the Fool and ending with the World. These cards are almost always fully illustrated, no matter what tarot deck you use. They're typically associated with the "big" themes of life and borrow from

archetypal meaning-making systems from around the world.

Some of the more recognizable cards you might have seen in movies and TV (like Death, the Lovers, and the Devil) are Major Arcana cards.

MINOR ARCANA

This is the collective name for the fifty-six cards that make up the four tarot suits: Cups, Swords, Wands, and Pentacles.

These cards are often, but not always, concerned more with action and everyday choices than the Major Arcana, which tend to be more broadly thematic.

Some tarot decks might give the suits different names according to the creator's preference (Pentacles might be Coins or Discs; Swords are sometimes Knives; Cups may be Vessels; and Wands have many names, including Torches, Staffs, Batons, Staves, and Rods).

MEANING-MAKING SYSTEMS

"Meaning-making system" is an umbrella term for a spiritual, moral, or emotional text, tool, or set of beliefs that human beings look to in order to give meaning to our lives and experiences.

Jungian and Freudian psychology, astrology, religion, political parties, and of course, tarot, are all meaning-making systems.

"Meaning-making system" is a neutral term. It does not suggest that any set of spiritual, moral, or emotional tools, texts, or beliefs is right, wrong, good, or bad.

ORACLE CARDS

Card decks that don't follow the seventy-eight–card tarot formula aren't tarot decks. These might use other popular cartomancy systems instead, like Lenormand or Kipper systems, which are both made up of thirty-six cards. Other decks may have their own unique system invented by the individual deck's artist. These are typically referred to as oracle decks.

You can absolutely use oracle decks, Lenormand and Kipper cards, or even runes and playing cards for the spreads in this book, but note that the prompts and content within this book are based on tarot.

SPREAD

This is the combination of tarot cards laid out on a table (or floor!), with each card correlating to a specific meaning. Spreads give the cards additional context and narrative shape.

The simplest, most classic spread is "Past, Present, Future," in which three cards are drawn: one to represent the past circumstances around a topic, one to represent the present circumstances, and one to represent the future opportunities. (This simple spread can be great for writers plotting character arcs or entrepreneurs ready to take the next step for their business.)

Many tarot readers will have go-to spreads they like to use (Past, Present, Future is definitely one, and so is the ten-card Celtic Cross featured in Appendix II), but for the sake of creativity, I encourage you to create your own.

For example, a musician looking for ideas for their next song might improvise a two-card spread, with the first card representing the message they want to convey through the lyrics, and the second card representing the mood or energy of the sound.

In this book, every card in the deck includes a simple spread inspired by the theme of the card. There is also an appendix of additional, more complex spreads at the back of the book. If you want an example of how to read a spread, head on over to Appendix I.

TAROT SYSTEMS

There are thousands of different tarot decks out there with unique artistry, but there are two primary traditions that most tarot decks tend to draw their foundations from: the Marseille system and the Smith-Waite system.

The Marseille system is, generally speaking, the less visually intricate of the two. While the Major Arcana are fully illustrated in Marseille decks, the Minor Arcana are minimalistic—a Six of Swords card, for example, depicts six swords, and nothing else. While there is a lot to appreciate about the Marseille tarot tradition, I don't typically recommend Marseille decks for beginning readers, folks practicing intuitive reading, or anyone looking to use the tarot for creative purposes; in my experience, the Marseille's Minor Arcana lack the rich symbolic cues present in more modern systems.

The Smith-Waite system, rooted in Pamela Colman Smith's illustrations for A. E. Waite's 1909 deck, is probably the most mainstream and recognizable tarot tradition.

All seventy-eight cards are fully illustrated, with each Minor Arcana suit telling its own compelling visual story.

Most modern decks by contemporary artists will be looking to one of these two traditions to inform their work, but many indie decks take liberties—both for the sake of artistic license and to make the tarot's imagery more inclusive of race, gender, and body type. Lisa Sterle's Modern Witch Tarot modernizes and diversifies the cast of characters from Smith's twentieth-century deck, while Claire Burgess's Gay Marseille updates the Marseille style with gender and sexual diversity.

This book's interpretation of the tarot is rooted primarily in Pamela Colman Smith's system (also known as the Rider Waite Smith deck, or, as it is referred to in this book, the Smith-Waite deck). My choice to rely on the Smith-Waite imagery is practical (the deck is readily available for readers around the world), creative (the depth of detail in the Smith-Waite system offers so many opportunities for inspiration and unique interpretation), and personal (my first deck was a Smith-Waite, and it feels like my first language as a tarot reader).

A Note on Gender in the Tarot

Traditional tarot symbology has struggled to keep up with society's evolving understanding of gender expression and roles. For many years, certain cards have been defined as squarely "masculine" or "feminine," and many traditional interpretations of archetypes like the Emperor, Empress, and each suits' Kings and Queens have been flattened by reductionist gender norms. That said, there is plenty of gender fluidity within Smith's original tarot artwork: some cards, like the Fool, Justice, and the Pages, are notably androgynous. The World dancer has historically been read as intersex by many tarot readers. As usual with the tarot, everything is up for interpretation, including the gender identities of the tarot's cast of characters.

In this book, while I have opted to keep the traditionally gendered titles of Empress, Priestess, Emperor, King, and Queen to maintain continuity with most tarot decks, I have chosen to use gender-neutral pronouns to refer to every character in the tarot. Not because the tarot must be genderless, but because I believe the tarot, and every character within it, should be left to the interpretation and creative license of the reader. You are allowed, entitled, encouraged to see masculinity, femininity, and everything in between in each card, but I want to leave that up to you. I want you, regardless of your gender, to feel free to see yourself in every figure of the tarot.

Gender these cards in whatever way feels right to you; feel free to change your mind in different circumstances. You are empowered to play with the spectrum of gender as you develop a relationship to the cards. Remember that above all things, the tarot is a crucible for creativity—you get to use your own imagination and instincts when it comes to these characters' identities.

PART I

Your
Creative
Heroes

The Major
Arcana

THE TWENTY-TWO MAJOR ARCANA cards traditionally represent major archetypes, common facets of the human experience.

Starting with the Fool, and ending with The World, these cards can be used individually for reflection, idea generation, and meditation. They can also be read in sequence as what many tarotists call "The Fool's Journey"—a cyclic, archetypal storyline following the universal experience of moving from naivety and innocence toward transcendent wisdom—and all the ups and downs and evolutions along the way.

The cards in the Major Arcana sequence offer valuable creative tools. They can stand in for characters, customers and clients, goals, themes, muses, and plotlines, and can be assets that help us both ground and expand what we already know about the projects we're working on.

Personally, I like to use the Majors in two ways: as creative prompts and as reflective tools. Each is equally important in this book, because only through reflecting on ourselves can we fully access the freedom of expression that we need to turn creative prompts into something exciting, satisfying, and unique, both for ourselves and for the future audiences of our work.

As creative prompts, the cards help me explore the energy, themes, and cast of characters involved in my writing projects. I can use them to identify and profile characters when I'm still in the broad strokes phase of drafting. I've seen artists use the Major Arcana to prompt tone and theme in their work, dancers turn to the body language of each Major Arcana character to inspire movement, and songwriters use the Major Arcana to set the mood for their compositions.

Tarot cards can be so creatively generative because they offer us a channel for speaking our truth. Traditionally, many tarot readers have focused on the truth of our secrets, of our futures, of our love lives. But I think the juiciest truths are the ones we slowly peel back the layers of in our art, and tarot offers us a special shortcut to get there.

Of course, the cards do help us uncover truths about ourselves and our lives, too, and this can help us better understand ourselves as artists. When drawing cards for self-reflection rather than idea generation, I like to think of the Major Arcana as my creative patrons, my heroes: energetic investors in my work, steering me in the right direction and helping me stay afloat. Whatever I'm working on, tuning into the energy of a Major card helps me focus, reconsider, and unstick myself from creative ruts and fears. In other words, the Majors are my creative support system. They are the found family I carry around in my pocket and consult, whether I'm trying to remember my voice, come up with my next big idea, conquer a new theme in my work, or support myself through all the many highs and lows of my creative life.

The Major Arcana can be your creative heroes, too—you just need to get to know them.

Take Creative Risks

with

O

the
Fool

You know that feeling when your stomach flips over just as you crest the big hill of a roller coaster? The same one you get when a new crush leans in for a first kiss, or when a novel throws a shocking yet totally satisfying twist your way?

That feeling you get when a new creative idea lights your whole brain on fire and you eat it, sleep it, dream it until you finally put pen to paper or brush to canvas or fingers to keys?

That's the Fool.

The Fool represents the ideal creative state. Typical illustrations of the card show a figure with their head held high, facing the sun, lightly packed, and ready to leap into adventure, to be carried wherever the wind takes them.

But the Fool also shows up to remind you that to get that reward, you have to take that risk. To access the creative freedom you crave, you have to be willing to jump blind and see where you land. After all, the card makes no promises about what happens once the Fool steps off that cliff—maybe they'll sprout wings, maybe they'll fall, maybe there's a parachute in that little bag of theirs . . . there is just no guarantee.

The magic of the Fool is that taking a risk opens up a million new options and learning opportunities. The Fool may not know what's coming next, but they're willing to move forward anyway.

Free Your Mind

The Fool shows up as a motif within creative work across the spectrum; innocence, levity, and light are some of the essential, primary colors of creativity. Romeo and Juliet are quintessential Fools; so too are *Legally Blonde*'s Elle Woods, Will Bloom, the hero of *Big Fish*, and *Moulin Rouge*'s Christian (apparently Ewan McGregor makes a perfect Fool).

Even cynical or tragic works of art need the contrast of Fool energy (remember how Romeo and Juliet ended!), so it's good to know how you relate to this card—to recognize where its energy crops up in your work and how.

When the Fool comes up in a spread, it's often an invitation to free yourself up or to introduce an element of unbridled freedom into your creative work. Boldly dare to infuse bright colors or bubbly textures into your creations. Give one of your characters a devil-may-care attitude and see what that does for your story. Photograph the view from a cliffside, or imagine the world through the simple, joyful eyes of a favorite pet, and see what kind of art that outlook inspires.

Creative Prompts for the Fool

Write a story or poem about conquering a fear of heights. You might include an unexpected twist at the end that requires a leap of imagination for your reader.

Create a self-portrait that reimagines you as the Fool. Think about what jumping into the unknown means to you, and how you can illustrate that visually.

Make a mood board of your favorite vistas and write a poem about each view over the next month.

Journal about what creative freedom means to you. How close do you feel to that feeling, and how can you alter your environment to create a freer creative experience for yourself?

The Fool Spread

To make a more personal connection with the card and dive deeper into what creative risk-taking means to you, use the following spread to explore the creative support the Fool has to offer.

Turn to this spread when you're feeling creatively dry, burned-out, blocked, or lost. Shuffle your deck, then look through and find the Fool. Lay out the three cards behind the Fool as answers to the questions in the spread. Reflect on how each card relates to the question.

·✳ 1 ✳·	·✳ 2 ✳·	·✳ 3 ✳·
Where do I need more creative joy in my life?	What risk do I need to take to access that joy?	How can I help myself be brave enough to take this risk?

Manifest Your Ideas

with

the
Magician

When Salvador Dalí was commissioned to illustrate his own version of the tarot in 1973, he created a Magician card in his own image—an incredibly bold and clever act of manifestation. "This is my world," he seems to say through the card. "My vision."

Like Dalí, you can embrace the confidence-boosting energy of this powerful card.

All you have to do is accept your role as the Magician of your creative world. This takes preparation and practice. Notice that the Magician stands before a table covered with tools, including the symbols for the four suits of the tarot (the cup and sword are the most obvious, but the plate-like shape on the far left could represent Pentacles, and the flaming object in the Magician's right hand, Wands). Unlike the Fool, this card is not about jumping in blind, but about gathering your skills, tools, and ideas with intention.

Magicians conjure opportunity; they make things happen for themselves. They exercise their own agency. And that's the kind of energy it takes to bring your creative dreams into the world.

Bring It All Together

The inclusion of all four tarot suits in the illustration is important to reflect on. It takes a combination of material resources and supplies (Pentacles), passion (Wands), intuition and emotional engagement (Cups), and critical thinking (Swords) to bring your creative vision to life. The Magician knows that each of these ingredients is a creative building block, but that only when these elements are brought together can a pursuit really find ground.

When the Magician appears in a spread, it could be encouragement to surround yourself with the things you need to fuel your creativity. This might be physical—Virginia Woolf didn't write about having a room of one's own for nothing. But it might also be about your mental and emotional environment. Is it a safe, empowering place? If not, what tools do you have to make it so?

By putting the right tools at your disposal, you're empowering yourself to create. Think of laying out your table and preparing your space as a magic spell, a method of summoning your ideas. Observe how the Magician's posture resembles a lightning rod, with one hand pointing to the sky and one pointing to the earth; this figure is a conduit for creative magic—and you can be, too. Taking action to supply yourself with everything you need is the first step in manifesting your ideas.

Creative Prompts for the Magician

Imagine the Magician's life story, as if you were hearing them tell it in the first person. What choices have led them to their current life, and how do they relate to those choices? What do they want now? Craft a character for a short story, novel, film, or play based on this fictional biography.

Paint, sketch, collage, or photograph a still life work of art that captures the tools you need to pursue your artistic ambitions. If you want to challenge yourself, create a whole series that depicts you using these tools.

Choose your own medium. Whether you prefer abstract visual art or song writing, brainstorm how you can capture the energy of this card through your chosen medium and style. How can you manifest the act of "making magic"?

Journal about a moment when you felt like you were making your creative dreams come true.

The Magician Spread

Use this spread anytime you have a creative idea you want to manifest.

Shuffle your deck, then flip through to find the Magician and pull it out of your deck. While you look at the card, shuffle again and lay four cards out to correspond to each position in the spread. Reflect on how the cards connect to the questions asked within the spread.

··❋ 1 ❋··

How can I take creative action right now?

··❋ 2 ❋··

What resources do I need to take creative action?

··❋ 4 ❋··

How can I plan ahead for where this action will lead me?

··❋ 3 ❋··

Where do I need emotional support while I take action?

Find Creative Depth

with the

High Priestess

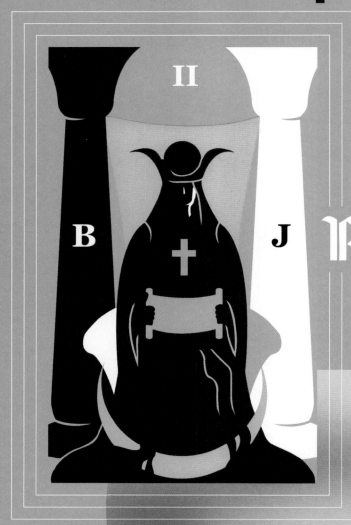

The High Priestess is one of the most mysterious cards in the tarot.

There's a dreamlike quality to the card, maybe due to the lunar motif that dominates the image. Notice how the priestess's dress and head are adorned with full and crescent moons. Water, an element that has an important real-life connection with the moon, is often depicted in the background art of this card (though not in the example shown here). In the tarot, water often represents our emotions and our intuition, while the moon can represent secrets and strangeness. Looking at the card's rich use of water and moon symbols might bring to mind that well-known phrase "still waters run deep."

Think of this card as a prod to reconnect to your rawest creative self—to your stillest, deepest waters. To soak up and spend time with your own mysterious but potent creative soul.

The High Priestess is all about looking inward, observing yourself. Understanding yourself. It's a nudge to be still and listen, to come to the cards without seeking a solution, but more as a means of meditating.

Get Below Your Own Surface

The High Priestess has long been linked to the myth of the Greek goddess Persephone. The story goes that Persephone spends half the year in the Underworld, and half the year above ground with her mother, Demeter, a goddess who rules over the harvest.

Symbolically, this myth represents the balance of withdrawal and action—as a creative, you need time to descend into your depths and contemplate your experiences and ideas as much as you need the flurry of making. Think of your creative process as the cycle of submerging into *yourself* to find what you really want to say through your creative work and emerging to share that message with the world.

To bring the High Priestess into your creative efforts, you need to consider what's lurking beneath the surface of your work. What subtext is driving your creation? What hidden gems are you layering in, and how can those hidden gems help you reveal the heart of your creation?

The card is also traditionally associated with "psychic" abilities, so it's a fun invitation to play with how intuition, instinct, and even the supernatural factor into your work.

Creative Prompts for the High Priestess

Spend some time in your own depths through meditation. Set a timer or use a playlist or soundscape online and spend at least ten minutes observing your thoughts. See if you can trace your surfacing thoughts to their emotional roots as they arise. Proceed with empathy and curiosity and see how deep you can go.

Write or illustrate a portrait of someone who matters to you with the goal of getting beneath their surface. Rather than describe or illustrate them physically, try to capture the essence of who they are as a person.

Craft a written or audio essay about an experience that defines your emotional landscape. How can this story help others understand you as a human being? How can it help you understand yourself?

Journal about your relationship with spirituality and ask yourself if you have a good grasp on what it means to be in touch with your own soul. How do your spiritual life and your creative life intersect—or how would you like them to?

The High Priestess Spread

Use this spread anytime you're feeling blocked or disconnected from a creative project. It's a great one to use if you're revisiting a project after a long break.

Shuffle your deck, then flip through to find the High Priestess. Pull out the card behind it, and place that card on your table, to correspond to the top card position in the spread. Shuffle again and repeat this process for each card position. Then reflect on how each card offers insight into the questions asked in the spread.

··✳ 1 ✳··

What do I want to say through this creative project?

··✳ 2 ✳··

What does this project want to say through me?

··✳ 3 ✳··

How can I integrate both when I create?

Cultivate Your Creative Environment

with
the
Empress

In most traditional tarot readings, the Empress represents the mother of the person being read for, mother figures in their life, their own role as a mother, or their relationship to the idea of motherhood more generally.

Creatively, this is rich territory—after all, the mother figure is a potent archetype in all kinds of art forms. Mary, mother of Jesus, is the art world's quintessential mother; the goddess Venus, with all her fertility and femininity, comes in at a close second.

Through historical examples like Seneca's *Medea*, Shakespeare's Gertrude and Lady Macbeth, and the evil stepmothers of the Grimm Fairy Tales, as well as the contemporary characters and themes in *Keeping Up with the Kardashians*, *Gilmore Girls*, *Crazy Rich Asians*, and *How I Met Your Mother*, it's clear that popular art will never tire of dissecting, redefining, subverting, and rehashing the figure and theme of "mother."

Art from every century, every culture, every medium is deeply invested in exploring everything a mother can—and in the minds of some artists, can't—be. Hopefully it's not too Freudian to say we're all probably doing some element of this dissection in at least one thread of our creative practice. And who could blame us? It's heady terrain!

The Mother of Invention

While mommy issues can be ripe for creative inspiration, this card is about more than family dynamics; it harkens back to the most ancient mother archetype: Mother Nature, Mother Earth. When the Empress appears, it's a call to examine the wider environment we create and exist within.

In traditional depictions of the Empress, you'll see a feminine figure who is completely at home in their environment. But that's thanks to more than the natural beauty of the landscape; there's luxury here, too—from the Empress's fine robe and star crown to her cushioned chaise. Effort has been made to make this a lush environment. Care and thought have been put into what the Empress needs to be comfortable, and the Empress glows with pride for having made a space for themself.

While the Magician prompts you to take ownership of your creative environment—to make it functional by giving yourself access to the tools you need to summon creativity—the Empress will help you turn that environment into the nurturing, fertile space your creativity needs to thrive.

When the Empress comes up in a reading, take it as a sign that some part of your creative project or some part of yourself needs to feel safe and loved. Look to the card's visual cues around comfort, spaciousness, and warmth to explore your own creative comfort. Then think about how you can provide yourself with a space that embodies those supportive sensations.

Creative Prompts for the Empress

Write a script or short story that puts a famously maligned mother figure from history or literature in the driver's seat of their own story. How can you use this character to explore, embrace, and subvert the Empress image?

Sketch your ideal creative environment. Hang this where you can regularly see it and make a plan to bring one element of your vision to life in your creative space.

Create a series of photographs, paintings, sculptures, or poems that explore what the archetype of mother, or the experience of motherhood, means to you.

Journal about three ways you could act as a good nurturer to your creativity.

The Empress Spread

Use this spread often—once a week, or even every time you sit down to create.

Without shuffling, spread your deck out on your table and draw two cards at random. Lay them out to correspond to the positions of the spread. Then reflect on how each card can offer insight into the questions asked by the spread. Make note of one action you can take immediately to nurture yourself or your work, based on what you learn from the cards.

··✳ 1 ✳··	··✳ 2 ✳··
What do I need to do more of to cultivate a nourishing creative environment?	What do I need to do less of to cultivate a nourishing creative environment?

Build a Creative

Structure

with

the Emperor

For many modern tarot readers, the Emperor can be a spiky card, and rightly so—the traditional imagery is patriarchal, colonial, authoritarian.

Those themes, of course, can be ripe for creative projects. Many enduring works of art and literature are meditations on the creator's relationship to patriarchy, empire, authority. And hell, if those elements of the Emperor are sparking a creative response in you, you have my full permission to throw this book face down on the closest surface, run to your creative space—be that desk, studio, garden, kitchen (or, if you're like me, most sunken corner of the sofa)—and start making something. But, if you're up for it, as a thought experiment, consider setting aside this card's worst associations and allowing yourself to find the creative support it does have to offer. Because while everything they say about The Emperor's rigid, unemotional, authoritarian attitude is true in many contexts, when it comes to creativity, this card can actually help us cultivate a healthy relationship to structure.

How Do You Relate to Structure?

The Emperor is assigned the number four in the Major Arcana. In the tarot, fours are associated with stability, solid foundations, safety, and structure.

In your creative life, structure can play the role of the benevolent boss—an authority figure who actually helps you on your path, who gives you the space, the support, and the safety net to grow.

Structure means different things to different people, and every creative person—often every creative project—has a different relationship to it. That means that the Emperor, in a creative context, is no dictator. They are a defender and supporter of the systems that work for *you*.

Working with the Emperor can mean investigating and reframing your relationship to structure. It's about finding ways to create stability in your creative life that feel good and generative for you, respecting your own personal rules, boundaries, and systems, whatever that means for you.

When the Emperor comes up, it's asking you a simple question: How do you build a space, a schedule (or intentional freedom from a schedule!), a way of working that allows your creativity to thrive?

Creative Prompts for the Emperor

Look to architecture as an art influence. Sketch, photograph, paint, or otherwise recreate a building in your local area. Notice the structure, form, and shape of the building, and play with that structure in your artwork.

Explore the energy of the Emperor card in poem, song, or video set to music. How will you structure the piece to make it most effective?

Draw a past, present, future spread and write a story or script based on the cards you pull. Doing this will help you implement structure into your writing by giving you clear dots to connect.

Journal about the structures that help you create, or brainstorm new ways of structuring your creative process that work for you, instead of against you. Remember that the structures that worked for you in the past don't have to stay forever. You are always free to adjust and adapt the way you approach your creative work.

The Emperor Spread

Finding structures that support your creative process can completely change your creative life. Use this spread to help you reflect on and start to build structures that work for you.

Simply shuffle your deck and split it into four piles. Take a card from the bottom of each pile (the foundation of the stack) and lay them out in the spread. Then reflect on how the cards respond to the prompts in the spread.

··✳ 1 ✳··

How do I benefit from creative structure in my life?

··✳ 2 ✳··

Where do I need freedom from structure in my creative life?

··✳ 3 ✳··

How can I be more playful in my approach to creative structure?

··✳ 4 ✳··

How can I build meaning-ful, supportive structures into my creative life?

Seek Out Creative Mentors with

V

the Hierophant

The Hierophant card depicts the Pope, or a Pope-like figure. In the Marseille system, the card is actually called "Le Pape." But don't assume this card promotes piety or a specific religious doctrine—it's a lot more than that.

The word "hierophant" entered the tarot lexicon in 1909, when the creators of the Smith-Waite deck opted to distance the card somewhat from the Church. They kept the Catholic imagery but chose to rename the card using an ancient Greek word that more broadly describes any leader of a spiritual congregation, someone with knowledge of or access to deep spiritual truths: hierophant.

The Hierophant can represent connection to a higher or deeper power. But it can also represent the experience of dealing with institutions, bureaucracies, and systemic gatekeepers. After all, the Pope isn't only an intermediary between humanity and divinity, but also a figurehead for the vast institutional functions of the church.

Learn from Others, but Trust Yourself

You don't need an intermediary to access the secret depths of your own creativity. Instead, the Hierophant can be a huge help when you're dealing with creative institutions. If you're looking to turn pro in fields like publishing, design, and curation, or trying to start your own creative business, then having a mentor to help demystify the process can be critical to your success. So, rather than seeing the Hierophant as a spiritual intermediary, think of this card as an invitation to seek out mentors and friends who have been through the creative experiences you want to embark on.

Just be wary of putting these mentors on a pedestal. While it's helpful to have advocates and guides along your creative path, the truth is that your journey is unique. No creative ever took the same exact road as their peers, no matter how much support they received on their own journeys.

When you remember that no one in your creative life gets to gatekeep your creativity, and that many successful creatives have found their way completely independently, you may discover that it's not a mentor you need at all: It's your own direction that is most valuable to you.

Ultimately, the Hierophant represents an opportunity to investigate how you're being led and by whom. Where do you need direction and guidance? And who is most suited to give that guidance to you: someone else, or your own self? It's up to you to decide.

Creative Prompts for the Hierophant

Write a letter to a creative mentor from your past and let them know what you took away from the relationship, both good and bad. Use this as an opportunity to reflect on how you've evolved in your creative practice, thanks to, or despite, your experience with your mentor.

Create a piece of art based on an imagined religion. Write a story or develop a piece of visual art about an imagined belief system. What kind of iconography does this imaginary religion lean on? Who are the leaders? What kind of people follow it?

Create a portrait of your ideal mentor or leader. Use words, music, or visual media to experiment with how you can express the feeling of working with your ideal mentor. What kind of advice do they give, and how can you illustrate that sentiment through art?

Journal about the ways you can be a mentor to yourself. How can you support your own growth as a creative, and how will that self-reliance inform your creative path?

The Hierophant Spread

Understanding the kind of creative leadership you need can sometimes feel like a daunting task, but this spread is here to help you explore and get clarity around what you're looking for.

Shuffle your deck and draw three cards. Lay them face down on the table in front of you and turn them over one by one. Then reflect on how the cards respond to the prompts in the spread.

··*1*··	··*2*··	··*3*··
What do I need from a creative mentor?	How can I seek out the mentor I need?	How can I be my own creative mentor?

Commit to Your Creativity

VI

with the Lovers

While the Lovers is no guarantee for a happily-ever-after, many readers typically do associate the card with romance—and why shouldn't they? It's right there in the name.

Love, of course, is one of the most timeless themes for creatives. Nothing is more creatively invigorating than the promise of new—or renewed—love. On the flip side, a need to understand and heal heartbreak can be a compelling creative impetus, too. If love inspires you to make your art, you're in good company. Almost all of Shakespeare's plays make love their muse. The Beatles' love songs made them the top-selling recording artists of all time. Gustave Klimt's fantastical, glittering homage to love, *The Kiss*, is one of the most recognizable paintings in the world. The "Modern Love" column in the *New York Times* has captured the hearts of readers for twenty years. And romance novel sales continue to grow and grow. It's undeniable: Love is the creative gift that never stops giving.

But there's more to the Lovers tarot card than fodder for dreamy visuals, delicious pop songs, and delightful rom-coms. And of course, there's more to love than that, too.

Are You a Good Partner to Your Creativity?

The Lovers card is really about partnership. About the choices and commitments you make to the things you love. It's not a card about *falling* in love. It's a card about sticking with what you love through better and worse.

When you think about your longest standing partnerships, you probably think of friends, or romantic partners, or even work collaborators.

But your relationship with your creativity is a partnership, too. Learning to treat it like one could be game-changing for your creative life. For one thing, seeing your creativity as a partner will empower you to find new ways of working with it. For another, approaching experiences of creative block the same way you might address a conflict with a friend or loved one will help you show compassion to yourself and focus on working toward meaningful solutions. And finally, looking at your relationship to your creativity as a partnership will foreground the importance of making commitments to maintain and nurture your creativity.

Whenever you draw the card, think of it as a chance to reflect on how you're honoring your commitment to your creativity, or how you might want to review and revise the creative commitments you've made.

Creative Prompts for the Lovers

Create a piece of art that illustrates an ideal partnership. Think about what that means to you, and how you might use metaphor and tone to convey the elements you most value in partnership. Consider how these values are present in your relationship to your own creativity.

Recreate this card using a visual medium you've never worked in before. Paint, watercolor, cross-stich, clay . . . the world is your oyster. But whatever medium you choose to work with in recreating the Lovers card, make sure you fully commit to giving it a go, no matter how self-conscious you feel while trying something new.

Write a vow of fealty to your creativity. In the Middle Ages, knights swore oaths to the noblemen and women they served. What would an oath to your creativity read like? Consider the vows you can confidently make, the commitments you won't break, and put them down on paper—or turn your words into a spoken performance piece.

Journal about what you want from your creativity as a partner, and what you offer your creativity in return.

The Lovers Spread

Reflecting on your relationship with your creativity as a partnership can sometimes be a challenging mindset shift, but don't worry—the tarot is here to hold your hand while you do this work.

Use the spread that follows to regularly check in on your partnership with creativity and identify what's working, what needs to change, and how you can work together toward your dream creative life. Simply shuffle your deck, draw three cards, and then reflect on how the cards respond to the prompts in the spread.

* 1 *

How am I being a good partner to my creativity?

* 2 *

How is my creativity a good partner to me?

* 3 *

How can I deepen my commitment to my creativity?

Compose and Trust Yourself

with
the
Chariot

The Chariot captures a moment that will feel familiar to anyone who's ever undertaken a passion project: This card is the breath before you dive into the deep end, that moment of pause before the beautiful but chaotic experience of going all in on something that matters to you.

We join the charioteer in the final moments before takeoff. They're almost ready to go, but not quite on their way. The sphinx steeds haven't yet been reined to the Chariot, and the wheels aren't yet turning. The charioteer is taking this moment to gather their strength, their vision, their drive to go onward. No matter how much you're dying to get on the road, this card serves as a reminder that it's wise to take advantage of that crucial sliver of calm before the creative storm to compose yourself and be present in the now.

Take Stock of Your Past, Your Present, Your Future

The Chariot shares some strong visual motifs with a few cards that have come before it in the Major Arcana sequence. The black and white sphinxes and charioteer's armor mirror the High Priestess's pillars and moonlit robe; the charioteer also wears a crown of stars reminiscent of the Empress's starry headdress and carries the same white wand as the Magician. By invoking similar imagery to these earlier cards, the Chariot reminds you of how prepared you are for the next step: You've mastered skills like confidence, faith, intuition, and nurturing.

But the Chariot doesn't just echo cards that came before—it also shares visual language with cards that come later in the Major Arcana— most notably the Wheel of Fortune. In the Wheel of Fortune, a wheel turns, and a sphinx sits on top, a reminder that while we are always subject to unexpected fate, we can also steer ourselves through surprises, good and bad.

When the Chariot comes up in a reading, take a deep breath. Reflect on where you are now, how far you've come, and how prepared and capable you are for what's next. Wherever your creativity is leading you, take this moment to ground yourself in the faith that you're going in the right direction, and you have everything you need. Now exhale and put yourself out there.

Creative Prompts for the Chariot

Create a vision board about a creative project you want to start. Think about what images, quotes, and other elements will give you the fuel to make the thing you want to make.

Write a story or poem or short script that uses wheels as a motif. What does it mean when wheels are spinning, versus when they are still, versus when they're broken? Use wheels as a metaphor to hint at your characters' feelings.

Use a riddle as artistic inspiration. In mythology, sphinxes often speak in riddles; do some research and find one that captures your imagination. Create a piece of art in the genre of your choice that illustrates or explores the riddle. Or try creating your own original riddle.

Journal about a moment in your life when you were on the precipice of pursuing something important. What spurred you forward, and what held you back? How did it feel when you finally committed and went for it? How could recreating that energy in your life now be useful for you?

The Chariot Spread

This spread is a twist on the classic Past, Present, Future tarot spread. It invites you to take a moment to reflect on your vision for the future so you can move forward with intention.

Shuffle your deck seven times, while taking deep breaths. When you're done, take the first three cards from the top of the pile and lay them face down in front of you in the pattern that follows. Then reflect on how each card answers its prompt.

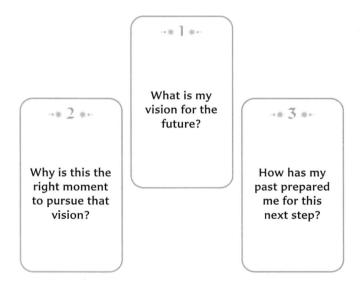

·＊ 1 ＊·
What is my vision for the future?

·＊ 2 ＊·
Why is this the right moment to pursue that vision?

·＊ 3 ＊·
How has my past prepared me for this next step?

Do Hard Things

with

VIII

Strength

Living a creative life is not always fun and games, even though we strive for playfulness as much as possible. Sometimes, we come up against moments that feel anything but playful. Moments that can stretch into streaks that feel hard and scary and even insurmountable.

The hard things are different for everybody— some people struggle with criticism of their art and some struggle with praise. Some artists create their most honest work when in the throes of painful feelings while other creators shut down when they hit rough patches in their personal lives. You might get a thrill promoting and selling your work, or you might clam up at the idea of allowing anyone to see something you've created. You might love starting something new but struggle to finish it, or you might dread the early days of figuring an idea out, but love bringing everything together in a project's final stages.

Whatever challenges you, remember that the difficulties you personally encounter in your creative life are valid; you're allowed to find some aspects of your creative existence hard. Luckily, the Strength card is here to hold your hand as you face the scary stuff and ultimately come out the other side a more confident, resilient creator.

Your Heart Is Your Strongest Creative Muscle

When you think of strength, you might think of physical strength: big muscles, heroic feats of athleticism. But true strength runs deeper than that—your own heart can be your biggest source of strength.

The traditional illustration of Strength emphasizes courage over brawn: In it, a finely dressed maid uses bare hands to gently pry open the jaws of a lion. A lemniscate, or infinity symbol, floats over their head.

It's hugely important that centuries of tarot artists have chosen such a tender display to represent the archetypal energy of Strength. It's a reminder that true strength requires a certain level of vulnerability and sweetness in the face of difficulty. Being soft and open is a crucial skill for getting *real* with the hard things.

When this card comes up for you, see it as a prompt to practice resilience, the quieter sibling of strength. Cultivating resilience requires gentleness and guides you to approach difficult moments in a way that honors the experience you're having.

Seek out ways of working that prioritize openness, curiosity, and beauty over the brute force of a "just get on with it already" attitude (often our first response to encountering something hard). Consider how you can hold your own hand through it, how you can really get to the heart of it, how you can honor yourself and find sweetness alongside the difficulty.

Creative Prompts for Strength

Practice yoga or breathwork today. Explore how moving your body can make you feel not just physically strong but also creatively strong. How does the combination of gentleness and effort mirror your creative process? Consider turning your observations and connections into art, be it dance, film, or a piece of writing or visual art that captures the experience.

Write a short story about a character faced with an incredibly hard thing and the surprisingly gentle way they respond to the challenge. Keep it short, sweet, and powerful.

Create a collage using magazine cuttings of words and phrases that indicate emotional and creative strength to you.

Journal about what kinds of experiences in your creative life feel "hard." Note any patterns. Forgive yourself for any ways you feel you've fallen short when faced with creative challenges and consider how you might respond with more sweetness for yourself the next time you face a hard thing.

The Strength Spread

This spread is here to help you reflect on the difficult moments you face in your creative life and summon the strength you need to move forward.

All you have to do is shuffle your deck and then flip through until you find Strength. Pull out the two cards directly behind it and lay them down in the pattern that follows. Then reflect on how the cards respond to the prompts in the spread.

·❋ 2 ❋·

What can I do to find sweetness while I do the hard thing?

·❋ 1 ❋·

What hard thing do I need to face in my creative life?

Follow Your
Creative Vision

IX

with the
Hermit

When you draw the Hermit, you might be initially tempted to think, "Oh, I get it. I need to cut myself off from everything and everyone and get the project done." But that knee-jerk reaction doesn't really reflect the full picture of what the Hermit is saying to you and why.

While the Hermit *is* about doing your own thing, it's not necessarily about shutting yourself off from the world. The card's traditional illustration depicts a figure on the road, not cooped up at home. The Hermit isn't hiding from the world—they're exploring it. But they're not interested in following any map; rather, they're guided by their own inner light.

That confident curiosity is the card's true magic—it's a call to adventure. It's Gandalf showing up at Bilbo Baggins's door, Morpheus offering Neo two pills, Robert Frost beckoning you to take the road less traveled. The Hermit is a call to action, not a shelter-in-place order; recognizing that will make all the difference for your creative journey ahead.

Protect What Lights You Up

When the Hermit comes up in a reading, you're invited to ditch maps and directions and go on your own journey instead. Eschew what you're being told is the "right" way and trust your gut. Keep your creative process sacred, personal, sometimes even secret. Give yourself the gift of a creative adventure on your own terms, rather than remaining trapped in someone else's version of what your creative work, process, or life should look like.

That's not to say that you should never take feedback. After all, the tarot itself is a form of feedback. It means you shouldn't yield to feedback that extinguishes the light of your vision.

The Hermit wants you to respect what keeps your creativity burning, and follow *that* light instead of chasing after the approval or attention of anyone else. It's not a card about *forcing* yourself to be alone, but it is a card about owning your creative vision and doing what feels right for you, even if that means going it alone.

Creative Prompts for the Hermit

Go on a solo trip and record the experience. The trip can be short or long—a half-hour walk or a two-week holiday. And you can use any medium to record your journey: photographs, diary entries, letters, daily vlogs. Don't share any of these recordings with anyone until the trip is over and you've had time to reflect on your creations and what they mean to you.

Create your own Hermit's lamp. Make a 3D structure inspired by the lamp's shape and place an object inside it that represents your own inner voice. Keep your lamp in sight, to remind you to follow your own light and trust the path you're on.

Create a self-portrait that depicts you at your best. Use your own judgment as far as what "best" means. Don't rely on past compliments you've received. What does your vision of your best self look like?

Journal unfiltered about exactly what you're thinking and feeling in this moment. Tap into your stream of consciousness; take note of what happens when you just allow yourself to exist on the page. It may be uncomfortable at first, but practicing this regularly can really help you tune in to what you truly need and want to express.

The Hermit Spread

This spread is here to help you check in on the opportunities and obstacles facing you while you work with Hermit energy.

Shuffle your deck until your instincts tell you it's time to stop shuffling. Then pull out four cards and lay them out in the pattern that follows. Reflect on the message that comes through the spread.

> ·•· 1 ·•·
>
> What creative journey do I need to take on my own terms?

> ·•· 3 ·•·
>
> What can I do to stay my own course?

> ·•· 2 ·•·
>
> What barrier might get in the way of my light?

> ·•· 4 ·•·
>
> How can I invite others on my journey without getting off track?

Navigate the Unexpected

with the

Wheel of Fortune

The Wheel of Fortune captures a dilemma that creatives face all the time: the complex and often contradictory relationship between fate and will, between embracing the unknown and bringing a vision to life.

Let's start by looking at the name and the primary feature of the card: the Wheel of Fortune, a symbol associated with luck and big twists of fate. Creatives will recognize this archetype: Like the ever-spinning motion of a wheel, our creativity turns and spins to its own logic. Sometimes ideas come; sometimes they go. Motivation comes and goes, too. The reception of our work gives us highs and lows. Things rarely stay the same for long, and much of our creative experience can feel out of our hands. We have to give ourselves over to fate and enjoy the ride.

I personally love the four-winged figures in the corners of this card—an angel, an eagle, a bull, and a lion. All four recline on clouds, and each is busy writing in a book. There's a comforting reminder here: I may get thrown off the Wheel and flung somewhere unexpected, but wherever I land, I know I'll be able to write about it. I'm going to make sense of my experiences through expression. Embracing the truth that I'm a creative even while fate is messing me around has been a huge relief to me in times of upheaval.

Where's Your True North?

While a come-what-may attitude can be freeing, accepting whatever fate and fortune throw your way is not the whole lesson of the Wheel of Fortune. Look closely and see for yourself: The Wheel's design doubles as a compass.

Compasses help you orient yourself when you're lost. Tune in to a compass, and you'll uncover true north; you'll get a sense of where you are and where you want to go. Developing your inner creative compass, a sense of faith in and reliance on what your gut is telling you to create, is a crucial tool for navigating the unexpected things life throws at you.

If the Wheel is both a device for making you dizzy and a device for finding your way, then its lesson is that learning to orient yourself requires facing the unexpected. You only understand what it's like to know where you're going if you understand what it's like to be lost.

Yes, the Wheel keeps you endlessly spinning, endlessly guessing. But your experiences navigating whatever the Wheel of Fortune throws at you will help you uncover the course you really want to follow. Slowly but surely, you'll learn to return to your true north—the creative spark that keeps you going, no matter where in the world fate sends you.

Creative Prompts for the Wheel of Fortune

Draw, paint, or collage a compass that represents the different directions you navigate as a creative. Feel free to get abstract here—what does a compass or map of your own creative experience look like?

Write a story or script about someone trying to find their way. Illustrate several of the situations they encounter on their journey, and imagine that each one has the potential for both a happy and an unhappy ending.

Imagine what each of the four figures in the corners of the card is writing in their books. How does each figure's unique personality come through what they are writing or sketching?

Journal about what true north means for you as a creative. What are the fundamental truths of your creative identity? What subjects, styles, and genres do you return to again and again?

The Wheel of Fortune Spread

The unexpected elements of living a creative life can be disorienting. This spread will help you face the unknown while staying true to your creative core.

Shuffle your deck and draw three cards, laying them out in the pattern that follows. Then reflect on how the cards relate to the prompts in the spread.

1

What is fate throwing at me?

2

What message is my creativity sending me now?

3

How can that message help me through the unexpected?

Check Your Privileges and Margins

XI

with Justice

The majority of this book provides tools for looking inward and examining your own creative landscape to find inspiration and fulfillment. But the Justice card invites you to peek out of your individual creative cocoon and participate in a wider discussion about the experience of creatives around the world, and the role creativity can play in building a more just world.

The concept of justice has always been a rich subject for creative expression. Sophocles's classic play *Antigone* (and many of its modern adaptations) explores the injustices of war. The writings of Hannah Arendt and James Baldwin are beautifully crafted meditations on justice. Justice has long been a compelling theme for documentary filmmakers, most street art is rooted in justice movements, and conversations around justice have been brought to life through music and dance for generations.

Your creativity can be a powerful tool to help you fight for the world you want to live in. Using your art to call for justice, whether that's by meditating on the theme in your work, offering your creative skills to activist groups, connecting to other artists who share your values, or finding other creative ways to act in service to a more equitable world, isn't just the right thing to do; it can also be creatively invigorating.

It's important to recognize that for many creatives, there's an inherent privilege in being able to prioritize your art—sometimes in identifying as a creative at all. Arts funding and education have become a luxury in even the wealthiest countries in the world, and access to jobs in the creative industries consistently favors the wealthy and well-connected. While creativity is inherent in each and every one of us, not all of us have the opportunity to nurture our creativity. That's a terrible injustice, one that is up to us, as creatives, to fight against.

Rebalance Your Own Power

The imagery in the Justice card is a nudge to consider your relationship to power and privilege. Several symbols stand out: the scales, the sword, the crown. This figure is in a position to make judgments and take action, so it naturally invites you to reflect on what privileges you have as a creative, as well as to consider the power dynamics that exist in your creative life.

When the card comes up, it's asking you to measure your privileges and your margins, to explore the power you have to make a difference, to identify the areas where your creative experience is marginalized, and to commit to actions you can take to fight for creative justice, and for justice in your world writ large.

Creative Prompts for Justice

Offer your creative skills to a local charity, nonprofit, or activist group. That might mean designing a logo for your local women's shelter, teaching art classes for an after-school program in an under-resourced area, raising money for a cause by selling your work, or anything else that serves the organization you want to help.

Create a piece of art in any genre that explores what creative justice looks like to you. Look for inspiration in the work of creatives whose own commitment to justice plays a crucial role in their art.

Choose a social issue close to your heart and write an essay that reflects your own opinion and experience with that issue. Consider how your words could impact others dealing with this issue.

Journal about ways you can contribute to a more just world. Reflect on where you most want to see change, and what opportunities you have to fight for it.

The Justice Spread

To create a more just world, you first need to be intimately aware of your own privileges and margins. This spread will help you reflect on where you need help versus where you can give help, and how you can take action in support of justice.

Shuffle your deck and draw three cards. Lay them face down on the table in the pattern that follows and turn them over one by one so you can give each individual card your attention before moving on to the next. Reflect on how each card relates to its prompt.

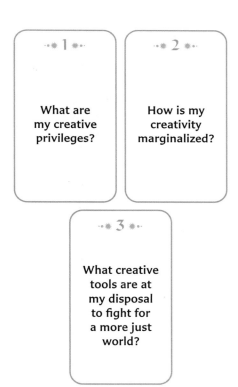

· ✳ 1 ✳ ·

What are my creative privileges?

· ✳ 2 ✳ ·

How is my creativity marginalized?

· ✳ 3 ✳ ·

What creative tools are at my disposal to fight for a more just world?

Surrender Control

with the

Hanged One

Here's one tarot myth I've always wanted to bust: The Hanged One hasn't been hanged as in executed. The central character in this card is alive and well, even if we're meeting them in a strange position. Look at most versions of the card from the Smith-Waite and Marseille traditions and you'll notice that the figure is suspended from a tree *not* by the neck, but by the ankle. The rest of their limbs are free, and their body language is relaxed. Their facial expression is totally serene, and a golden halo is glowing around the character's head.

The main character of this card is thriving in their unconventional environment. They're taking in the world from new angles and finding pleasure in the experience. This is not an all-is-lost moment—this is a *welcome* plot twist.

The Hanged One paints a picture of an essential element of the creative process: that moment when an unexpected, unconventional, even weird scenario results in enlightenment or inspiration. This card is the manifestation of those ideas that come seemingly unbidden in the shower, on long walks, on your commute, or while you stare out the window when you "should" be working. The truth is that those ideas aren't unbidden at all. You've summoned them in by giving your mind the space and freedom to wander.

Allow for Vulnerability

The martial artist and filmmaker Bruce Lee famously said that creativity is "a process of surrender, not control." The Hanged One encapsulates this value.

To welcome new ways of seeing, the Hanged One is surrendering themself to the unknown—to a way of seeing that literally turns their world upside down. This requires radical vulnerability, a quality that you need in spades if you want to live a creative life. Finding creative solutions is all about suspending yourself in the unknown, receiving the experience and responding to it, instead of planning out the process from start to finish. When this card comes up in a reading, you're being asked to open up and cede control. To make yourself vulnerable, to surrender yourself to whatever strange, unexpected, and seemingly unbidden creative impulses come your way.

Creative Prompts for the Hanged One

Take yourself somewhere you've never been—a new coffee shop, a new city, or a new route to work. Don't try to "create" while on this journey. Just engage with the experience as fully, presently, and curiously as possible. When you get back home, make note of three interesting things that happened on your journey. Do this every couple of weeks and notice how your capacity for attention and curiosity evolves.

Make a work of art that imagines something or someone you love from an unexpected point of view. Write about your dog from the perspective of his favorite toy; snap photographs of the soles of your most well-worn shoes; mix up your favorite outfit by bringing in a new piece.

Write a poem in reverse. Start with the last line, or try out reverse rhyme (make the first words of each line rhyme with each other, instead of rhyming the last words of lines).

Journal about a time you saw someone close to you in a new (positive) light. What did you learn about them that you hadn't known before, and how did that help your appreciation for them grow?

The Hanged One Spread

Lean on this spread when you need help letting go of your need for control.

Shuffle until a card naturally jumps out of the deck. Take your time observing that card—really look at it from every angle, and allow yourself to be surprised by new observations that come with looking differently. Then reflect on how that card answers the prompt that follows.

·※ **1** ※·

How can surrendering control fuel me creatively right now?

Kill Your Darlings

with Death

No one can agree on who coined the phrase "kill your darlings." The quote's been attributed to William Faulkner, Allen Ginsberg, Eudora Welty, and Oscar Wilde. Whoever said it, generations of creatives have taken the advice to heart.

Boiled down, to "kill your darlings" is to be willing to move on, to let your old ways die and embrace new challenges. What's more, it's about actively pursuing opportunities outside your comfort zone. Following this advice means committing to evolution, even when—or maybe especially when—it would feel safer to stay where you are. To kill your darlings is to embrace change, challenge, discomfort. It's to strive for what's next, what's better, what's unknown.

Working with the Death card in a creative context is the same. Death is a prompt to jettison what's safe and easy and pursue the difficult, challenging next steps on your creative journey.

Give Yourself over to Discomfort

Neither the Death tarot card nor the advice to "kill your darlings" should be taken literally. Death and murder are mere metaphors for change, harbingers of a possible life—and creative satisfaction—beyond everything you thought you knew.

No one is asking you to set fire to the home you lovingly decorated, put your poems in the shredder, give up on your dream of running a creative business, or even kill off a beloved character in your screenplay. But confronting the theme of death is a transformative rite of passage that will undoubtedly up your creative game.

Death demands that you give yourself over to discomfort in service of growth. Kill your darlings by leaving your comfy nine-to-five to finally pursue your dream of freelance illustration. Embrace metaphorical death by junking the manuscript you've been tinkering on for a decade and starting something new, or by rewriting the story from scratch in the first person rather than the third. Prune your garden so that new flowers can grow (feel free to take that one literally or metaphorically). Release whatever vision you had of what creative success is supposed to look like and instead follow your gut toward what creative satisfaction *feels* like. Kill your quaint ideas of what "good" is and find out what lies beyond. Give yourself permission to step into a new version of yourself and let the old you fade into the background.

When the Death card appears, it's time to make a change. Let your past expectations, hang-ups, hopes, and fears die so that there's room for new, beautiful possibilities to come to life.

Creative Prompts for Death

Write a letter to a past creative project that didn't work out how you hoped. Thank it for what it taught you and give yourself permission to move on.

Create a piece of art in any medium that captures your idea of what the best-case-scenario afterlife looks like.

Make a list of old creative ideas you're hanging on to because you're afraid to move on, or because you feel responsible for completing them even though the idea no longer fires you up. Give yourself permission to ignore them for the next year. You don't have to kill them entirely, just remove any expectations for now. Imagine what new, exciting things you're making room for instead.

Journal about the version of yourself you'd most like to be. How can you kill off old expectations and hang-ups so that you feel free and ready to step into this new, evolved version of you?

The Death Spread

If you need an accomplice to help you kill your darlings and rise from their ashes, trust this spread to be your partner in crime.

Shuffle your deck, then flip through until you find the Death card. Pull out the three cards behind it and lay them face up in the pattern that follows. Reflect on the message that comes through the spread.

··✳ 1 ✳··
What habits in my creative life do I need to put an end to?

··✳ 2 ✳··
What unhelpful thought pattern about my creativity needs to go?

··✳ 3 ✳··
How can I be kind to myself and my creativity while I make change?

Avoid Creative Burnout

with
Temperance

Once upon a time, craftspeople had long phoneless days to hone their skills; artists spent hours sketching their favorite paintings in museums; novelists weren't under pressure to create viral tweets to promote their books while simultaneously rushing to keep pace with publishing schedules; and poets had the quiet, unpolluted darkness of long nights to let their words take shape. We don't have the same luxuries today.

Don't get me wrong, the present moment offers some incredible creative opportunities. The internet has paved the way for more diverse and accessible creative expression, and tech innovations have led to boundary-pushing creative work in art, film, fashion, gaming, business, and more.

But there's no denying that when we're constantly on the go and under pressure to deliver creative work and solutions, the time and space we have to actually be creative shrinks. And the time and space we have to *enjoy* our creative process threatens to disappear.

When we force ourselves to power through and create at breakneck pace, it all too often leads to the buzzword of our generation: burnout.

That's where Temperance comes in.

Refresh Yourself

This is a card about moderation and conservation. The angel in the image has paused to refresh themself, to dip their toes in cooling waters, and to contemplate the healing properties of rest.

That Temperance comes up between two tough cards—Death and the Devil—in the Major Arcana sequence is no accident. Temperance buffers the hard stuff by providing a moment of soft, slow refreshment. It's a much-needed, much-deserved sliver of light in the darkness.

Temperance is a call to take a pit stop, to make space for daydreaming and recovery.

The card challenges you to reframe your creative journey as a steady jog that you want to sustain over the course of your whole life, not a quick sprint. Practicing the values of temperance in your creative life—learning how to take breaks, make the most of what's available to you, and stop pressuring yourself to do the next hard thing *right away*—will help you to understand your creativity better and foster more meaningful creative work in the long run.

When you draw the Temperance card, take inspiration from the moments in your life when you've given yourself permission to pause and rest.

Creative Prompts for Temperance

Stop what you're doing right now and go pour yourself a glass of water. Seriously. Drink the water. Slowly. Thoughtfully. Don't look at your phone, don't flip through this book. Just sit with the sensation of this small gesture of care and healing.

Design a mood board collage that makes you feel calm and gives you permission to go slower—in all areas of your life. Include the colors that make you feel calm, the kinds of environments that relax you, the quotes and poems that put you at ease. Put on a soothing playlist and take as much time as you need.

Write a letter to yourself from the point of view of the angel in this card. What would they tell you about taking care of yourself and your creativity? What advice would they give to help you achieve the cool comfort they emanate?

Journal about a time you recovered from, or managed to avoid, burnout in the past. What strategies did you put in place? What care did you offer yourself? Who did you look to for help? Keep this reflection in a place that you can easily access it in case you need it, like a burnout first aid kit.

The Temperance Spread

This Temperance-inspired spread gives you the tools to reflect on the elements of your creative life that may be pushing you toward burnout, and to take a meaningful moment of pause and refreshment.

Take three deep breaths to center yourself before shuffling your deck and laying three cards out in the pattern that follows. Reflect on how the cards you draw respond to the prompts in the spread.

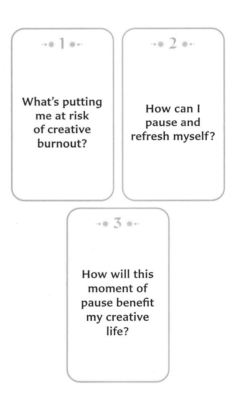

··✳ 1 ✳··
What's putting me at risk of creative burnout?

··✳ 2 ✳··
How can I pause and refresh myself?

··✳ 3 ✳··
How will this moment of pause benefit my creative life?

Stop Self-Sabotage

with
the
Devil

Traditionally, the Devil has been linked to vice, addiction, and the consequences of "bad choices." In other words, the Devil brings your own personal demons to the surface; it forces you to confront the many ways in which you jeopardize your own happiness, comfort, and success. It's the pitch-perfect illustration of what self-sabotage looks and feels like: a trap, with no apparent way out.

In your creative life, you sabotage yourself when you dismiss an idea as "bad" before you even try to explore it. When you overcommit. When you obsess over your follower count or sales figures instead of nurturing your creativity. You sabotage yourself when you procrastinate, when you water down what you really wanted to say, when you waste years waiting for the permission of teachers, critics, peers, and industry insiders to show up as your most creative self.

You also sabotage yourself when you beat yourself up for all that self-sabotage.

The Devil card challenges you to unshackle yourself from a cycle that keeps you in the dark, separated from your freest, healthiest, most satisfying creative life.

The Devil Is in the Details

In the Smith-Waite tarot tradition, the illustration captures two figures chained to a stone block. Perched on top of that block is a demonic vision—the kind of creature that belongs in horror movies and bad dreams.

But the real devil is in the details of this card: Look closely at the chains around the figures' necks and you might be surprised to find that these collars are loose. This is the uncomfortable truth of the card: You have the ability to free yourself from your demons; you just have to be willing to seek out the gaps in your chains and squeeze through them. You have to want to escape the things that are holding you back from feeling creatively satisfied.

Not every barrier that keeps you from creating is self-imposed—socioeconomic factors, cultural norms, health conditions, and other external issues may always create battles for you in your creative life and may require greater systemic shifts to open up creative avenues. But when the Devil appears, see it as a nudge to examine the specific ways you're holding yourself back, and start looking for holes in the fence.

Escaping your own self-sabotaging habits won't be easy, but realizing you have the power to rewrite your story is half the battle, and the Devil gives you the opportunity to change the narrative right here and now.

Creative Prompts for the Devil

Make a list of ways you self-sabotage in your creative life. Give each of these "demons" a silly, unthreatening name (my procrastination is called Lloyd, and my perfectionism is called Skarfdingus). When you feel them start to prey on you, call them by their silly name and let that lighten the tension.

Write a script for a short film or stage play that puts the scene of the card into action. Give personalities to all three figures involved, the humans and the demon, and make their interactions—and the outcome of the script—*funny*.

Create a work of visual art that uses chains as a motif. Think of the chains you encounter in your everyday life, both metaphorical and literal.

Journal about a time you found your way out of a hole you'd dug yourself into. Reflect on what this experience taught you.

The Devil Spread

Every creative person will self-sabotage at some points along their journey. Don't be ashamed if you're struggling; turn to this spread to help you find a way out and to affirm yourself while you seek to end this cycle.

Shuffle your deck while imagining your mind filling with a warm, golden light. When you're ready, draw three cards and lay them out in the spread that follows. Then, reflect on how the cards you draw relate to the prompts in the spread.

·· ✳ 1 ✳ ··

How am I sabotaging myself in my creative life?

·· ✳ 2 ✳ ··

Where can I look for a way out?

·· ✳ 3 ✳ ··

What is an affirmation that will give me hope while I end this cycle of sabotage?

Embrace the Worst-Case Scenario

Worst-Case Scenario

XVI

with the Tower

I'd love to tell you that living a creative life is all rainbows, sunshine, and orgasms. But sometimes, it's the pit of despair, and no tarot card understands and holds space for the worst things better than the Tower.

Whether you've lost your dream commission, had a devastating rejection from an agent, missed out on a job or promotion, received a diagnosis that significantly sets back your creative vision, or opened up your computer to find that, somehow, the draft of your novel has disappeared forever, there will be moments of your creative life where you feel struck down and smashed to rubble.

You will wonder how you'll ever build yourself back up again.

Facing a "Tower moment" in your creative life means encountering the worst-case scenario. This is not a card about love and light. It's a card about shock, devastation, and disaster.

But the Tower is also a beacon—sitting with the grief, fear, and desolation that this card conjures is the first step in choosing not to let hitting rock bottom be a death sentence.

This Too Shall Pass

I love that this card doesn't shy away from the drama and disaster of our darkest moments. The free fall depicted here is comforting in a weird way—it acknowledges the very real feelings of loss and wreckage that accompany creative failure. But this is not an image of *perpetual* despair; it's an illustration of the very worst moment, and a reminder that we have a choice in how we pick up the pieces.

The lightning strike is important, because it symbolizes that even the worst moments are flashes in the pan. They will do their damage, and leave you to crawl back to your feet, survey the wreckage, and rebuild.

When the Tower comes up, or when you seek out its advice, take the time to reflect on what's going wrong for you in your creative life. Give yourself permission to sit with the discomfort, the pain, the fear. Allow yourself to have that moment of grief, to respect the devastation. Take stock of the damage and let yourself feel it. You can't start to heal and rebuild until you've confronted the damage and made space for your pain.

In fact, getting a sense of what's broken and giving yourself permission to feel it can be creatively generative. Your experiences may open up new ways of seeing, new things to express, new inspirations to create.

Being struck by lightning can be the worst thing that's ever happened to you, but it can simultaneously be an electrifying current that sends you off in meaningful new directions.

Creative Prompts for the Tower

Write a letter to your past self at a time when you were experiencing a worst-case scenario. Give that grieving version of you the gift of understanding and the promise of what you have been able to rebuild.

Write a story about two characters who come together after experiencing their own "Tower moments" in life. How are their experiences similar, how are their experiences different, and what will they learn from each other?

Break something—seriously. Then reshape the broken thing into a wholly new piece of art.

Journal about the ways you've seen people rebuild and create their way out of their worst moments. This might be people you know, public figures you admire, or beloved characters in books and films.

The Tower Spread

If you're facing a worst-case scenario moment, let this spread hold space for your experience and offer you options for rebuilding when you're ready.

Shuffle through your deck and select two cards. Lay them face down on the table in front of you, and turn them over one by one. Then, reflect on how the cards you draw relate to the prompts in the spread.

· ☀ *1* ☀ ·

How can I hold space for the pain I'm experiencing?

· ☀ *2* ☀ ·

Where can I seek out the strength I need to rebuild?

Reclaim Creative Self-Care

with **the Star**

"Self-care" as a concept has had a wild couple of decades. In tandem with the rise of social media and the wellness industry, it morphed from an important tenet of activism into a marketing buzzword. The Star card is an invitation to find your way through a maze of must-haves and must-dos and return to the heart of self-care: *yourself* and *your* care. It begs you to fill yourself up with what works for you, to pour out what doesn't, and to recognize that truly, deeply caring for yourself is not a day at the spa—it's challenging inner work.

The term "self-care" was popularized by the feminist writer Audre Lorde, who identified self-care as a crucial part of her activism and life as a Black lesbian woman. Caring for herself gave Lorde the strength to fight for change in the world, helped her heal the wounds she sustained while putting herself on the line as a public figure, prompted her to prioritize her basic physical needs and connect to her community, and guided her back to herself, to her identity as an artist and a writer.

For Lorde, self-care wasn't about self-improvement or self-soothing; it was about radical self-acceptance and self-prioritization in a world that told her she wasn't enough, that she didn't deserve attention or love. It was intimate, tailored to her own experience; it wasn't something she could order off a menu. It was something she created and cultivated.

Commune with Yourself

The Star, with its twilight scene of a nude figure kneeling beside a quiet pool, conjures up an intimacy, vulnerability, and attention that echoes Lorde's concept of self-care.

In the tarot, water symbolizes the subconsciousness; the figure in this illustration is communing with what's below their own surface and attending to the needs of their personal environment. This is nurturing; this is attentiveness; this is thoughtful, intentional, deep, and vulnerable care.

As a creative, communion with yourself as an act of care is essential. It can help you when you feel burned out, guide you toward the things you want to express through your art, support you when you face rejection, and inspire you to create a more meaningful practice.

Tarot, with its deeply reflective nature, is a wonderful self-care tool for creatives. So is journaling, gardening, singing, walking—whatever brings you closer to yourself.

When you draw this card, reflect on what your care needs are in this moment, and how you can honor them in an intimate, personal, thoughtful way.

Creative Prompts for the Star

Make a list of things that make you feel at peace. It might be something as simple as leaving your phone off for the first hour of the morning, going outside on your lunch break, or having a hot shower. Do at least one thing on this list every day for the next week and reflect on how you feel afterward.

Write a short story where a character finds a secret passageway to their own paradise. What do they do to protect it? How do they bring what they found back into the world with them?

Design a star that represents the themes of this card. Display it in your home or workplace where it can remind you to connect back to yourself and honor your care needs in the moment.

Journal about how prioritizing self-care impacts your creativity and how you'd like to deepen that impact.

The Star Spread

When you need support on your creative self-care journey, turn to this spread.

Shuffle your deck, then flip through until you find the Star. Lay out the four cards directly behind the Star in your deck, and place them face up in the pattern that follows. Reflect on how the cards you draw answer the questions in the spread.

·✴ 1 ✴·
What creative self-care need am I experiencing right now?

·✴ 2 ✴·
What can I do to meet that need?

·✴ 4 ✴·
What can I do to break through those barriers and give myself what I need?

·✴ 3 ✴·
What challenges might be in the way of my ability to meet that need?

Embrace Your Creative

Phases

with

XVIII

the
Moon

Scientifically speaking, the moon is a natural satellite of the Earth. Over the course of a year, it takes roughly twelve journeys around our planet. Each orbit lasts about twenty-eight days, and during that time we see many different versions the moon, based on how much light it's reflecting from the sun at any given point in its journey.

The moon we see in the sky changes, but the moon itself does not. It's always whole—we just don't get its full power all the time. At different times of the month, even different times of the day and night, the moon's influence on things like the tides varies depending on where the moon is in its orbital journey.

It can be wise to liken your creative journey to the lunar cycle. You, too, are always a whole creative person, whether you are actively making something or not. The moon doesn't always appear full to us, and you don't always need to be running yourself dry to create in order to claim the identity of artist, writer, creative, or whatever you want to call yourself. Recognizing the phases you go through on a regular basis, knowing how much energy you have for creativity throughout your days, weeks, months, and years, can be incredibly empowering.

What Phase Are You In?

The Moon card is about accepting the natural ebb and flow, the tides of your energy and inspiration. If moving through cycles of energy has worked for the moon for millions of years, then maybe mere mortals like us ought to accept that our attention span, energy, and abilities also wax and wane.

When this card appears, it can be an invitation to check in on yourself and identify what phase of your creative journey you're currently in. How full is your tank right now?

There's another element to the Moon card worth mentioning: strangeness, transformation, mystery. For as long as the moon has moved through its many phases in the sky, it has fascinated and inspired onlookers. Many people believe that the phases of the moon have profound effects on human behavior, and historically the moon has been linked to madness and recklessness. In a creative context, this interpretation could be a prompt to get a bit weird and wild, to make creative choices that feel "crazy" or mysterious, to let the light of the moon transform and shape-shift your art.

Creative Prompts for the Moon

Sketch out a comic strip or scene from a graphic novel that takes place by moonlight. How does the moon factor into the story and paint the characters and events in a different light than they might appear in daylight?

Write a poem or song from the point of view of the moon. Explore how the moon experiences its own phases, and how its orbit around the Earth affects the way it sees the world.

Draft a short story or film that takes place in eight parts and ends in a similar place to where it began. Use the eight phases of the moon as inspiration.

Journal about the common phases you experience in your creative life. When does your creative energy wax and wane? How can you learn to work with, instead of against, your patterns?

The Moon Spread

This spread can help you get clarity about the creative phases you're working with and embrace the weird humanity of it all.

Shuffle your deck and lay out eight cards face down. Then choose four of those eight and turn them over, laying them down in the pattern that follows. Reflect on how the cards you draw relate to the prompts in the spread.

···✳ 1 ✳···

A creative phase I'm stepping out of

···✳ 2 ✳···

A creative phase I'm stepping into

···✳ 3 ✳···

How to prepare for the next phase in my creative journey

···✳ 4 ✳···

Something weird and wonderful to embrace along the way

Believe Your Own Hype

with

the
Sun

The tarot's Sun is *radiant*. It shines more brightly, more boldly, than the Moon or the Star. It breaks open the sky with its brilliance, draws the sunflowers to attention, and illuminates the pure, unadulterated joy of the child at the illustration's center.

In the Smith-Waite tarot tradition, the sunflowers aren't facing the sun. Instead, they're facing out, soaking in the light of something even brighter.

That brighter thing is *you*, the observer of the card, the creator seeking guidance. And the Sun is here to remind you just how bright and brilliant you are.

This is a card about basking in your own glow, reveling in your own talent, achievements, and potential. It is permission—no, it's *instruction*—to buy into your own hype and give yourself a confidence boost.

It's natural to look for external validation for your creative endeavors. Whether you just appreciate the love or want to monetize your creative pursuits, the perception of your audience is undeniably important. But the Sun is here to remind you that buying into your own hype is a crucial part of bringing other people along on your creative journey.

After all, if you don't believe the sun is shining on your work, why should anyone else?

The Sun Takes Time to Rise

Many creatives struggle with believing in themselves. You might have been conditioned to equate confidence with ego; you might have had so many negative experiences that you can't imagine feeling good about or proud of your creative work; or you might be navigating anxiety or imposter syndrome or other valid mental and emotional barriers that affect your comfort when it comes to feeling and expressing pride and joy in your work.

The Sun is here to throw up a mirror to show you how brilliant you are and illuminate just how much you deserve to bask in the glory of your own creative gifts. When you draw this card, celebrate the parts of your creative life that you love. It might be things you've created, a part of your creative ritual, or a collection of compliments you keep on hand to remind you how great you are. The more light you shine on these things, the sturdier your foundation of confidence and self-belief will be.

As you work with the Sun, remember that believing in your own hype is a process—the Sun takes time to rise, too.

Creative Prompts for the Sun

Curate a sunshine playlist that makes you feel radiant. Put it on whenever you want to warm yourself up to a creative task, or anytime you need a creative energy boost.

Write a poem about how it feels to bask in the glow of the sun. Bring in specific memories you have of sunny days, and the emotions that being sun-kissed brings up for you.

Make light the focus of a series of photographs, sketches, or paintings. How can you put a new spin on illumination through your art?

Journal about what you think and feel when you look at the Sun card. What are your favorite aspects of the card, and what elements do you find most challenging? Consider how your response to the card mirrors your experience of shining a light on yourself and your creative work.

The Sun Spread

Believing in yourself is a journey. Turn to this spread anytime you need a confidence boost.

Simply close your eyes while you shuffle your deck, and imagine that sunlight is bursting out of your chest. Breathe into that feeling until you feel ready to come back to your cards, then select three cards from your deck and lay them out in the pattern that follows. Reflect on how each card you draw relates to the prompts in the spread.

·* 2 *·

What specific achievement should I shout more proudly about?

·* 1 *·

Where can I give myself more credit?

·* 3 *·

What is an affirmation for when I'm not feeling my own light?

Rediscover Your Creative Roots

XX

with

Judgment

The Judgment card takes its name from the biblical notion of Judgment Day. The book of Revelation envisions that when the world as we know it comes to an end, the Christian God will raise his true followers from the dead and create heaven on earth. The "judgment" refers to God's discernment of who he will and won't bring back to life.

But in my opinion and experience, the tarot is at its weakest when we chalk its symbolism up to rehashing religious tropes without entertaining what lies beyond the loudest parts of the card. So, when it comes to exploring this card creatively, I encourage you to drop the heavy-handed Doomsday vibes of the name (unless that gets you really inspired!) and look at it from other angles.

Personally, I *am* compelled by the imagery: The illustration of an angel singing the dead from their graves is undeniably potent. But I like to think of it less as a prophesy than a metaphor. In a creative context, the angel is you. The trumpet that rouses the dead is your creative practice. And the bodies rising up are the parts of you that you might have buried out of shame, fear, confusion, or simply in the course of growing up.

This is a card about bringing your full creative self back to life, about bringing up the good, bad, ugly, and everything in between that you've left behind on your quest to fit in, to be "good," to please others. It is not, despite its unfortunate name, a card about judging yourself, or your art, or others.

Stop Curating Your Creativity for Others' Consumption

When Judgment comes up in a reading, it can initially feel intimidating. And it is, but it's also beautiful. When I'm working with a client and this card appears, it immediately prompts me to ask them about what inspired them in childhood, or maybe just what connected them to their desire to be creative in the first place. Taking the time to brush the dust off your early creative desires and breathe fresh life back into them can be life-changing. This is especially true if you're recovering from perfectionism, or looking to reconnect to your rawest creative self after years of curating your creativity to fit what your teachers, boss, peers, or parents said creativity "should" look and feel like.

Working with Judgment is an opportunity to resurrect your purest creative joys, hopes, and ambitions, and bring them to life again. Just because you've buried them doesn't mean you've killed them off. You have the creative power to make yourself feel whole again.

Creative Prompts for Judgment

Make a creative time capsule. Intentionally bury some creative ideas and unfinished projects, then dig them up in three, six, or twelve months' time. Reflect on how your relationship to these ideas has changed in that time. Imagine how you might reconnect and push these ideas forward with a new perspective.

Script a short zombie film where the undead are creative ideas you abandoned out of fear or low confidence.

Write a poem or song that captures the feelings this card stirs up in you.

Journal about your earliest creative memory. Write to remember the freedom of your imagination in that moment, and explore the things that got in the way and buried that freedom over time.

The Judgment Spread

Turn to this spread to help you unearth the creative impulses you've buried and to reconnect to your true creative self.

Flip through your deck until you find the Judgment card. Remove it from the deck and set it aside. Shuffle, and then draw the first card in the spread from the bottom of the deck. Draw the second card in the spread from the top of the deck. Lay them both face down in the positions that follow and reflect on how the cards you draw relate to the prompts in the spread.

··✷ 1 ✷··

What creative impulse have I buried or deprioritized over time?

··✷ 2 ✷··

How can I bring that impulse back to life?

Make a Fresh Start

XXI

with
the
World

The World is the culmination of everything the Major Arcana has to offer. The imagery combines many themes explored through all the cards that came before. The nudity of the central figure captures the Star's vulnerability, while the wands in their hands hark back to the Magician, symbolizing creative power. The figures in each corner of the card mirror the winged creatures in the corners of the Wheel of Fortune.

This card offers a potential happy ending to the risky leap of the Fool in the very first card of the Major Arcana. The Fool advises you to take creative risks and trust the mysterious journey those risks send you on, even if it means falling off a cliff. But the World makes a promise: Master the lessons of the tarot, and you'll have everything you need to stay afloat and thrive in your creative life and beyond.

The connection between the World and the Fool is strong; they're two halves of a whole. You can only understand and access the World if you have the courage to take the Fool's leap, and the openness to learn from all the cards in between.

Get Ready for What's Next

For many tarotists, the Major Arcana is not a straight line from Fool to World, but a cycle or spiral . . . a path you'll continue to follow and learn from again and again. Reaching the World prepares you for your next journey, which will require a new Foolish leap.

In a creative context, the cyclical narrative of the Major Arcana can be hugely empowering. With every Foolish risk, you create a new World, you achieve a new level, and you prepare yourself to play the Fool again.

A creatively satisfying life is the combination of bold risk and meaningful reward, and you get to walk that journey for as many projects as you can create in your lifetime. You get to dive in scared and emerge victorious and transformed with every creative endeavor.

When the World appears, you're called to reflect on how your creative pursuits, risks, and challenges have paid off. What growth have you seen in yourself as a result of connecting more deeply and intuitively to your creativity? How have you elevated yourself since you last drew, or reflected on, the Fool?

It's also an opportunity to ask yourself what's next. Who are you now, in the moment, as a creative person, and what are you hungry for? You may find your appetite has changed since you last found yourself on the precipice of a new project or pursuit. You might be craving new horizons and hopefully you'll find yourself ready to jump into the unknown, equipped with the creative support system you need— in the tarot—to weather the journey.

Creative Prompts for the World

Make a mood board or collage that illustrates your creative world. What exists here? What is important? What do you want more of? Use this as an opportunity to reflect on what you've built, and what you want to do next.

Imagine your own fictional world and indulge yourself by crafting it from the ground up. Make maps, invent unique creatures and plant life, imagine what drives the economy and the politics of this imagined world. Then, conjure a character who has to take a big risk to make this world a better place.

Write a short story or script that follows the Fool on their journey through the Major Arcana and ends at the World. Which of the Major Arcana will you turn into characters that the Fool meets on their journey, and which will represent experiences the Fool must learn from to reach the World?

Journal about what you've gained in your *Tarot for Creativity* journey so far. What new creative worlds have you opened up through the tarot?

The World Spread

Use this spread anytime you're feeling ready to take a new step in your creative journey—it will help you recognize where you are, how far you've come, and where to put your energy next.

Shuffle the cards and divide them into four piles. Take a card from the top of each pile, and lay them out face up in the pattern that follows. Then, reflect on how the cards you draw relate to the prompts in the spread.

· ✳ 1 ✳ ·

What new creative risks am I more than ready for?

· ✳ 2 ✳ ·

What energy should I bring to this new adventure?

· ✳ 3 ✳ ·

What major achievements and/or lessons have led me to this moment?

· ✳ 4 ✳ ·

How am I a wiser version of myself than I was the last time I started something new?

MAJOR ARCANA EXERCISES

Exercise 1

Draw a Major Arcana card and reflect on what films, books, shows, or works of art it reminds you of. How might you incorporate the same themes this card brings up in other creative works into your own projects?

Exercise 2

Lay all twenty-two Major Arcana cards out on the table and pick two: The first should represent how you see yourself in this moment, and the second should represent where you want to get to on your creative journey. Reflect on what actions you need to take to bridge the gap between the two cards.

Exercise 3

Every time you pull a Major Arcana card, take a moment to use your imagination: Fantasize about what happened just before the moment depicted in the illustration, and what will happen just after. Let this exercise expand your personal understanding of the card and what it has to offer you.

Exercise 4

Use the Major Arcana as talismans for your creative projects. For every different project you're working on, select a Major Arcana card to represent it. Whenever you sit down to work on that thing, pull the card you've chosen out of your deck and set it where you can see it while you work. This ritual will help you connect to your project on a new level, and keep you focused.

PART II

Your Creative Toolbox

The Minor Arcana

NOW THAT YOU'VE MET YOUR creative heroes in the Major Arcana, it's time to put your creativity into action with the Minor Arcana.

The fifty-six Minor Arcana cards make up the majority of the tarot deck. Rather than dealing in lofty major archetypes, they're more likely to reflect the everyday experiences of being a human (and, of course, a creative) in the world. And they have an interesting creative history of their own.

Unlike the Major Arcana, the Minor Arcana of the tarot weren't always fully illustrated with scenes and figures. Before Pamela Colman Smith and A. E. Waite created the commonly used Smith-Waite deck in 1909, most tarot decks were designed in the Marseille style. These minimal Minor Arcana were more commonly called the pips, or pip cards, and favored a simplified illustration style similar to playing cards. For example, the Eight of Cups was depicted as—you guessed it—eight cups, with little to no further contextualizing imagery.

I've got nothing against a Marseille deck— they are beautiful, and there are plenty of gorgeous modern tarot decks in the Marseille tradition. I own a Marseille deck that was hand-painted by a local artist where I live in the South of France, and more than once I've called it my most prized possession. But, when it comes to applying the tarot to creative pursuits, the Smith-Waite tradition is superior in my book.

Smith's artistic interpretation of each card literally changed the game for tarot. Instead of relying on memorization and vague fortune-telling codes to interpret the cards, readers could use Smith's deck to take their tarot storytelling to a whole new level. Thanks to Smith, most modern Minor Arcana images invite us into the heat of action. They're a powder keg for intuition's spark. They are epic stories neatly packed into the palm of your hand.

Modern Minors will drag you, sometimes kicking and screaming, into their world. My advice is to strap in and enjoy the ride. These are the cards that will help you apply the rich knowledge of the tarot to any and every creative experience you encounter.

The Cups will be your emotional support system as you navigate the highs and lows of the creative experience. Whether you feel down in the dumps or want to celebrate your biggest wins, these cards are here to hold space for every feeling on the spectrum, and to help you find healthy ways to turn your strongest feelings into art.

The Swords are the cards to turn to when everything feels poised to break—when you experience the dizzying heights of creative doubt and fear. These sharp and spiky cards understand that sometimes living a creative life can feel like a battle, and they're here to fight the good fight right alongside you.

The Wands are the friends you need to cheer you on when you want to generate ideas, clarify your vision, and chase down your creative passions with fierce determination. This is the suit to call when you're ready to light your creative fire and get to work.

And the Pentacles bring all the creative energy bursting through the Cups, Swords, and Wands down to earth. These practical cards will help you make space in your daily life for creativity, and even turn your creative pursuits into viable business and career options. These cards are dedicated to helping you manage your creativity for the precious resource it is, so that you can stay grounded and sustain a long, healthy creative life.

In these fifty-six cards, you'll see many takes on the same themes: Each suit has its own point of view on when, why, and how to take breaks, deal with hardships like criticism and failure, and celebrate your creative wins. The Aces will give insight into harnessing the pure creative energy of each suit, while the Pages, Knights, Kings, and Queens will offer you a wide selection of creative role models to learn from. All the cards in between will hold space and offer advice on navigating highs and lows of living a creative life. Most importantly, each action-packed card has the power to ignite your creative imagination through the illustrated scenes on the cards, as well as through the prompts and spreads I've supplied for each card.

As you turn to the Minor Arcana, remember that these cards aren't here to read your mind or to give you a set of rules to follow. They're here to offer you a mirror and a map, an opportunity to get curious about your creative experiences and find new ways of thinking about your work.

Cups, Swords, Wands, and Pentacles are all tools—and so are these cards. Use them creatively, however you see fit, and trust that whatever you choose to do with them is exactly right.

The Cups

The entirety of the tarot functions as a tool for tapping into your feelings and exploring your inner creative life. But no suit does this with more emotional intelligence than the Cups, the suit of the heart, emotion, and mood.

In a creative context, the Cup cards collectively offer a framework for understanding how you feel about your creative work and your creative life. Some cards, like the Ace, the Two, and the Nine, are radiant, positive representations of the emotional highs you experience as a creative. Others, like the Four and Five, validate the more difficult emotions you'll face along your creative journey.

The Cups, more than any other suit, recognize the ups and downs of living a creative life, and each of the fourteen cards offers wisdom for making the most of those highs and lows and maintaining a positive relationship with your creativity even when you're down in the dumps.

These are the cards you want to call when you have good news, because no one will be more excited for you. They're also the cards you want to run to when nothing's going right, because no one can offer a warmer, more understanding resting place.

The suit of Cups offers lessons to help you build emotional resilience to support yourself in the many seasons of your creative life, and they will empower you to develop a more loving and compassionate relationship with your creativity.

Cups are vessels. They're holding spaces. They're deep wells. When you interact with these cards, remember that they're designed to hold you and your entire creative experience with love, not judgment. Allow yourself to feel safe and seen within these images.

Master Creative

Abundance

with
the

Ace of
Cups

The suit of Cups opens with a striking image of abundance: a goblet becomes a fountain, overflowing and filling up the sea, beneath a clear sky.

The imagery in the card knows no bounds: Everything just keeps coming. It's the perfect illustration of that magical experience that creatives chase: flow.

But flow is an elusive creature, and many creatives (me included) have a bad habit of waiting for the flow state to find us, instead of working toward facilitating flow for ourselves.

Working with this card as a tool is about finding ways to summon abundance—of ideas, of energy, of creativity—rather than waiting for inspiration to strike and fill you up at a moment's notice. Imagine, for a minute, that the hand presenting the overflowing cup isn't a disembodied gift from the universe over which you have no control. It's your own hand. You are giving yourself the gift of creative abundance.

Banish Scarcity Mindset

To master the art of living an abundantly creative life on your own terms, you'll first have to confront your scarcity mindset. In a nutshell, a scarcity mindset is the fundamental belief that your creativity and resources have a finite limit, and that this limit keeps you from achieving your dreams.

But here's the truth that becomes evident through the eternal fountain in the Ace of Cups: The limit you're afraid of doesn't exist. Rejecting the idea that unless you're in an idealized flow state you can't really be creative, and instead embracing the truth that creativity is everywhere, whether it feels magical at first or not, is the secret to mastering creative abundance with the Ace of Cups.

Believe you can—and already do—overflow with ideas, and you'll start to see ideas everywhere. Commit yourself to a lifestyle that nurtures your creative energy, and you'll find the motivation you need to attend to your project. See yourself as creative, and you will be. That's the Ace of Cups' promise.

Loving your creativity starts with giving it this positive foundation. Like a parent setting their child up for success, if you want your creative life to flourish, you have to give it love and sweetness like water and sunshine, and then you have to stand back and watch it come to life in its own way, appreciating it for exactly what it is.

Creative Prompts for the Ace of Cups

Write a poem or personal essay that tackles the theme of abundance. Draw inspiration from a moment in your life where you experienced a transformation, from thinking you didn't have enough to realizing you had everything you needed.

Make a list of things, experiences, places, and people that make you feel creatively abundant. Commit to spending time in the presence of these things, people, or places, or to recreating an experience that has made you feel creatively abundant in the past.

Snap a photograph or make a sketch of an image from nature that illustrates abundance to you. Reflect on what that image has in common with the Ace of Cups, and your own relationship with creativity.

Journal about your relationship to creative abundance. Is it a difficult thing for you to master? Think back to the moments in your life that undermined your sense of creative abundance, and explore what steps you can take to heal from those experiences.

The Ace of Cups Spread

Use this spread to open up new perspectives on what creative abundance can look like for you, or whenever you feel your scarcity mindset start to choke out your creativity.

Close your eyes and shuffle your deck while imagining every breath you draw in is infusing you with creativity. Then lay out four cards in the pattern that follows. Reflect on how each card relates to the question asked.

··❋ 1 ❋··

Where am I actually experiencing abundance right now?

··❋ 2 ❋··

How can I use the abundance I'm already experiencing to bolster my creativity?

··❋ 3 ❋··

What's keeping me from embracing creative abundance?

··❋ 4 ❋··

What can a more abundant attitude help me achieve?

Deepen Your Creative Connections

with
the

Two
of Cups

The most obvious theme in the Two of Cups illustration is romance. Two figures stand across from each other, looking deep into one another's eyes, each reaching out for the other.

For many tarot readers, this card symbolizes marriage, soulmates, a communion of like minds.

In a creative context, the card can be a cue to focus on your artistic partnerships.

Depending on how you work and what you're working on, your approach to creative partnerships will vary. But generally speaking, there are three categories: the partnership you have with your audience, the partnership you have with your collaborators or creative support system, and the partnership you have with yourself and your own creativity. The Two of Cups offers you a chance to consider each kind of connection with your full attention.

Attention is a key takeaway from this card. See the way the two figures gaze intently at each other? That's the kind of attention you want people to give your work, the kind of attention you want to share with your collaborators and those who support you, and it's definitely the kind of attention you want to lavish on your own work.

Cultivate Connection with Yourself and Others

The Two of Cups is about connecting more deeply to the people who really *get* you, and about taking the opportunity to understand and love yourself as a creative.

But the card doesn't just serve as a reminder to give more deep and loving attention to your creative partnerships; it's also an invitation to get clarity around the nature of these partnerships.

Rising up between the two figures and their cups is a symbol that dates back to ancient Greece: the caduceus of Hermes. Depicted as two snakes wound around a staff, the caduceus is associated with exchange and reciprocity. And because of its association with Hermes, the Greek messenger god, the symbol has become entwined with printing, publishing, and expression. In other words, the way you express yourself, and the role your partnerships play in that, is bound up naturally with the symbolism of this card.

So when the Two of Cups appears, it's offering you a mission: Connect with yourself so you can get clear about what you want to say through your creative work, lean on your cocreators and support system to lend an understanding ear, and then use what you've learned to deliver a meaningful message to your audience through your creative expression. Make those three things happen, and the deep connection and understanding offered through this card is yours for the taking.

Creative Prompts for the Two of Cups

Create a portrait of someone who really gets you and your creative vision. This might be someone you create with, someone who supports you while you create, or a creative person you'd love to partner with in the future.

Write a love poem to your creativity. Give your creativity your full, undivided love and attention, and see what you learn about yourself in the process.

Script and record a short film that captures what creative connection means to you. Explore how that applies to your creative process now, or how you'd like it to in the future.

Journal about how you can show the other creatives in your life—and your audience—that you understand and support them.

The Two of Cups Spread

Use this spread to help you find and nurture your creative partnerships.

Shuffle your deck and then flip through until you find the Two of Cups. Select the next three cards in the deck that come after the Two of Cups and lay them out in the pattern that follows. Reflect on how each card relates to the question asked.

··❋ 1 ❋··
How can I connect to my creativity today?

··❋ 2 ❋··
How can I connect with the ideal audience for my work today?

··❋ 3 ❋··
How can I connect with a fellow creative who gets me today?

Celebrate Your
Creative Achievements

with the
Three
of Cups

When was the last time you really, truly recognized your creative accomplishments?

Whether it was ten minutes ago or ten years ago, the Three of Cups has arrived on the scene to encourage you to throw your creativity the party it deserves, right here, right now.

The artwork, featuring three figures dancing amid a harvest cornucopia, perfectly combines the energy of the Ace and the Two of Cups: It's a portrait of abundance and connection, an illustration of supportive creatives celebrating all of the achievements and potential in their creative lives.

It's not a scene that many creatives play out in their own lives very often. Usually, celebration is reserved for big, external successes. The Gallery Opening. The Book Launch. The Film Premiere. The Ribbon Cutting Ceremony. These things are absolutely worth all the fuss and festivity they're awarded. But the little moments in your creative life deserve fanfare, too, and that's what this card, with all its joyous energy, wants for you.

No Win Is Too Small to Recognize

When the Three of Cups shows up in a reading, see it as an opportunity to reflect back on what's gone well for you in your creative life recently. Did you have a new, exciting idea? Put the finishing touches on a project? Did you connect with a fellow artist who inspires you, or get a new client lead? Did you write a single sentence or put down a single brushstroke that you're happy with? Maybe the thing worth celebrating is the simplest but most important thing you can do as a creative: getting to work, whether the outcome is good or not. Celebrate the run-of-the-mill wins with as much fanfare as you celebrate the glamorous ones. Stop waiting for big things to happen to feel worthy of celebration. And if you're struggling to see what you've gotten right in your creative life recently, turn to friends, family, and your creative support system to lift you up and direct your attention to all the reasons why you're great.

When the Three of Cups comes up in a reading, it's an opportunity to remember that, whether you celebrate with yourself or with others, your creativity is a gift, every day, and you deserve to enjoy it.

Creative Prompts for the Three of Cups

Design a poster to cheer yourself on in your current creative pursuit. Imagine you're your own biggest fan, standing in the crowd and watching yourself on your creative journey. Hang the poster in your workspace to remind yourself that you can be your own best cheerleader.

Sculpt, build, or paper-mâché a trophy, or design badges or stickers that you can give to yourself whenever you have a creative win— no matter how big or small.

Write a song or poem that captures what it feels like when you win in your creative life.

Journal about three celebration-worthy moments in your creative life. First, reflect on a big win and how you celebrated it. Then reflect on a small win and consider whether you took the time to celebrate or not, and how you felt. Then, write about a creative accomplishment you'd like to achieve in the future and how you'll celebrate.

The Three of Cups Spread

This spread is designed to help you find accomplishments to celebrate in your creative life, and opportunities to celebrate ongoing progress.

Shuffle your deck and flip through until you find the Three of Cups. Select the two cards directly in front of the Three of Cups and the two directly behind, and lay them out in the pattern that follows. Then, reflect on how each card relates to the prompt.

·*· 1 ·*·	·*· 2 ·*·	·*· 3 ·*·	·*· 4 ·*·
What have I recently achieved in my creative life?	How can I celebrate that recent achievement?	What do I want to achieve in my creative life next?	How can I celebrate the small steps that will help me reach that goal?

Reframe Creative Block

with the

Four of Cups

The Four of Cups is a card you can turn to when you feel stuck. Can you see your experience of creative block illustrated in the card? In the worn-out expression and tense crossed arms and legs of the central figure? Look at the way the character eyes the three empty cups lined up in front of them. It's clear they've been looking for answers in these cups for some time, without success.

What the figure doesn't see yet is the fourth cup, blooming out of the air like magic.

Now, I'm not saying that the perfect idea you need is suddenly going to appear like a fairy godmother. But this card does offer some magical medicine, because it's a reminder that you are allowed, even encouraged, to sit with your stagnancy, instead of trying to fight it off or ignore its presence.

Are You Stuck or Do You Need to Slow Down?

Sometimes, feeling stuck is an invitation to slow down, reconsider what you have, and let that bring you where you need to go.

If you entertain the idea that feeling stuck may have its uses, then the Four of Cups becomes a card about trusting your process. And about loving yourself through your process—even in the moments that you're not getting the output you hoped for.

Trusting your creative process is an act of love. When you lovingly trust your process, you apply patience, compassion, and forgiveness to yourself as a creative, and when you apply the same virtues to the project you're working on, you open up mental and emotional space for ideas to flourish. No, they won't come out of nowhere. But they will come out of your willingness to give yourself space, time, patience, compassion, and forgiveness.

Whenever you draw the Four of Cups, take its advice by getting curious about the places in your creative life where stillness could benefit you.

By reframing moments of block as opportunities for stillness, you can develop a deeper sense of presence with your work and think differently about those moments when flow doesn't come easy. So, every time you see this card, remember: Being stuck can be a block, or it can be an opportunity to recover and rethink.

Creative Prompts for the Four of Cups

Create a collage that captures what stillness means to you. Include colors, textures, and other visual and sensory elements that illustrate the positives of being still. Refer back to this whenever you feel a sense of stagnancy.

Paint, draw, or photograph a still life scene using items that you feel drawn to in your home. Pay attention to how it feels to express stillness through a visual medium, and how that might change your approach to sitting still.

Write a story about a character who stays in one place the entire time. How can you create a sense of movement and progress, even if the character never actually moves?

Journal about your past relationship with creative block. Look back on times when you've punished yourself, or avoided dealing with your experience of stagnancy, rather than lovingly sitting with the feeling. Make a pledge to do things differently next time, and write down three ways you can acknowledge your blocks with compassion and patience.

The Four of Cups Spread

This spread can help you tune in to what you need in moments of creative stagnancy, and to lean on these experiences to enrich, rather than prevent, your creative work.

To use this spread, create an atmosphere of calming stillness for yourself. Shuffle your cards slowly while focusing on your breath for one minute. When you're ready, draw three cards from your deck and lay them out in the pattern that follows. Then, reflect on how each card relates to the question asked.

··✳ 1 ✳··

Where am I feeling creatively blocked right now?

··✳ 2 ✳··

What can I learn from that sense of stuckness?

··✳ 3 ✳··

How can I be compassionate with myself during this period of stillness?

Navigate Rejection

V

Five of Cups

Rejection hurts.

But as a creative, it's something that you have to learn to cope with.

Creative work is always received subjectively, and the truth is that there will always be people who like how you express yourself, and people who don't. It's the nature of the creative beast, but that doesn't make it an easier pill to swallow.

What can help in softening the blow of rejection is the lesson offered through the Five of Cups.

One of the most powerful things this card offers is the simple act of acknowledging the pain you're experiencing as a result of rejection. The three spilled cups stand in for the opportunities you lose when you're confronted with rejection. That opportunity might be a sale, a job offer, a chance to publish, a meaningful contact, or anything else that you hoped to gain when showing up in the world as your creative self. By illustrating the sorrow that is felt when you lose what you had hoped for, this card can help destigmatize the grief and pain of rejection—and that, in and of itself, is the first step to coping healthily with rejection.

Rejection Can't Dry Up Your Creative Well

As devastating as it is to see those three cups spilled, you might have noticed they're not the only cups in the picture.

Behind the grieving figure, two cups stand, upright and ready for the mourner to turn around and see that not all is lost.

Even more than that, not far away from the mourner and the five cups, there's a river. It's possible, then, that when the grieving figure is ready, maybe once they've acknowledged their feelings, validated the pain they're experienced, and turned around to nourish themselves with what they do have left, they could take their empty cups to the river and fill them back up again.

Read this way, the Five of Cups becomes a lovely reminder that rejection, even when it's deeply painful, is only a temporary setback. While the spilled cups and the mourner's black cloak acknowledge the pain and sorrow of rejection, the standing cups and the river are there, too, as a reminder that you can carry on and bounce back, no matter how much you're hurting in the moment.

Creative Prompts for the Five of Cups

Make your favorite comfort food and share the recipe on your blog, newsletter, or social media, or simply with a loved one, along with a note about how this particular treat helps you comfort yourself through rejection.

Put on a sad song and dance it out. Get in touch with your body and allow the music and your movements to express how you're feeling about your most recent rejection. This is a great way to reclaim your autonomy and to find new creative connections through your sadness.

Write a poem or song inspired by how your most recent experience with rejection made you feel. Don't shy away from big feelings. Let yourself be as dramatic and devastated as necessary to get those feelings out.

Journal about a time when a rejection you experienced actually opened up an unexpected door. Reflect on what you learned from that experience.

The Five of Cups Spread

Use this spread to find comfort and hope when you're dealing with rejection, so that you can take better care of yourself and move confidently forward when you're ready.

Shuffle your deck and flip through until you find the Five of Cups. Then, select the two cards behind it and lay them out in the pattern that follows. Reflect on how each card relates to the question asked.

··✳ 1 ✳··

How can I acknowledge the pain I feel now?

··✳ 2 ✳··

Where can I seek opportunity next?

Rediscover Creative Joy

Joy

with the Six of Cups

Think back to a time in your life when you felt truly and completely creatively free. How old were you? What were you making? How does the feeling you had back then differ from your daily creative experience now?

Odds are, you've conjured a memory of a time before you felt pressure to perform a specific version of creativity. A time when your creative expression was a given, something you didn't question or edit in advance. You might feel a little bit (or a lot) homesick for that time; you might feel angry that you no longer experience that freedom. Or you might feel that you never really had it in the first place.

Whatever you're feeling, the Six of Cups is a card that invites you to return to—or create anew—a sense of sweetness, warmth, and generosity in your creative practice. This card is a cue to create from a place of confidence and innocence, rather than a place of cynicism or expectation.

Prioritize Your Inner Child over Your Inner Critic

Traditionally, the Six of Cups is a card that summons nostalgia and connects readers of the tarot back to their inner child. When you draw this card, let it bring you back to a time before your inner critic took the reins of your creative practice.

In the image on the card, one figure offers another a cup full of flowers; surrounding them are even more flower-filled cups. You can read it as an offering from your inner child.

This card wants to see you rekindle the joy of creative expression by giving yourself the gift of pure, no-judgment creative freedom, and allowing yourself to accept it. Looking back to a time before you felt any creative pressure will be an incredibly generative exercise, especially if you're feeling blocked on a project.

The Six of Cups also offers an interesting creative twist: This is the first time in this suit that you see a cup filled with something other than water. These vessels aren't just for drinking—they can be flowerpots; they can be gifts. They can be safe places to plant your ideas and nurture them to grow. In embracing childlike joy unburdened by logic or societal expectation, the Six of Cups becomes an invitation to be generously unconventional . . . and what is creativity, if not exactly that?

Creative Prompts for the Six of Cups

Paint, sketch, or collage a piece that illustrates the happiest moment from your childhood.

Write an essay that weaves together your greatest creative success as a child with your greatest creative success as an adult. Where are the parallels in these stories, and where are the differences?

Play with your favorite craft material from childhood. Make a macaroni necklace, cornstarch slime, a paper chain, a diorama, or any other childhood art project that felt fun for you as a kid.

Journal about ways you can reconnect to your inner child in your creative life more often. Choose one thing you can fit into your schedule this week—and do it.

The Six of Cups Spread

You can use this spread anytime you want to infuse more joy into your creative practice.

Close your eyes, shuffle your deck, and think about a joyful moment from your childhood. Then, draw three cards and lay them out in the pattern that follows. Reflect on how each card relates to the question asked.

··✳ 1 ✳··
What does my inner child want me to know?

··✳ 2 ✳··
What gift can I give my inner child?

··✳ 3 ✳··
How can I integrate my inner child's message into my creative life now?

Embrace Your Potential

with the Seven of Cups

There's a concept called the "paradox of choice," which basically posits that the more options you have in front of you, the less able you are to make choices, and the less likely you are to be satisfied with any choice you do ultimately make.

As creatives, we know this problem well: Staring at the blank page or canvas, the unformed lump of clay, the unfocused camera lens, or the still, silent instrument can bring on waves of discomfort and fear. In this moment, the art you are going to make is a bit of a Schrödinger's cat: everything and nothing, genius and failure, beautiful and ugly, resonant and misunderstood, all at the same time. In the creative paradox of choice, every path your imagination conjures up for you to follow is simultaneously a path to ruin and reward.

Often, block is rooted in the fear of everything that could be—all the good and the bad wrapped up in the big bow of "maybe." The fact that anything is possible can be daunting, and the Seven of Cups captures exactly that—possibility, potential, alongside the fear and exhilaration that appear when every option is open to you.

Give Anything a Shot

I like to think that the Seven of Cups is here to reminds us that true potential lies in giving something a shot. Giving *anything* a shot. The beauty of this card's illustration is that while the central figure is captivated by the mystery cloaked beneath the covered cup, each cup that has already revealed its contents offers something positive, something interesting. The figure may not yet have stumbled across the elusive "perfect" idea or method that hides behind the veil, but they have things to work with right in front of them. They just have to pick up a cup and drink.

The same goes for you. The paradox of choice ultimately stems from the idea that there is a "right" thing, and that given enough time and evaluation of the options, you'll choose correctly. But "creative" and "correct" are mutually exclusive ideals. How you choose to express yourself can never be right or wrong. All that's important is that you make the choice to do it.

So, what are you waiting for? Pick a cup, any cup, toast to the potential it offers you, and drink up.

Creative Prompts for the Seven of Cups

Write a story about a character facing their own paradox of choice. How will you, as the puppet master of the story, move your character forward despite their freeze-up?

Create a collage that captures your own version of this card. Picture the options available to you now, and use magazine, newspaper, or photograph clippings to put those options down on your canvas. Pay attention to what images you're most drawn to, and reflect on how that helps you decide how to move forward.

Make a list of at least seven things you'd like to accomplish in your creative life, or creative ideas you'd like to pursue one day. Write out each item on a slip of paper, place them in a jar, shake it around, and pull one out. Commit to pursuing this creative achievement for at least one day, and see where it takes you.

Journal about your experience with paradoxes of choice. When do you feel overwhelmed by potential, and when do you feel compelled by it? Explore how your relationship with choice, commitment, and potential have played out in the past, and how you want them to play out in the future.

The Seven of Cups Spread

Whenever you're feeling overwhelmed and frozen by a paradox of choice, you can turn to this spread for guidance.

Shuffle your deck and draw four cards. Lay them out in the pattern that follows. Then, reflect on how each card relates to the question asked.

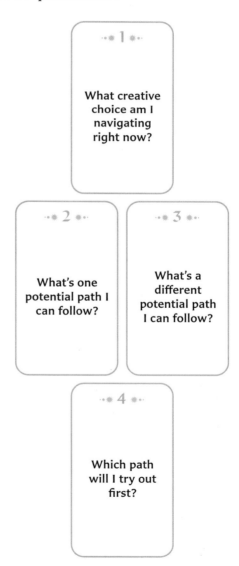

··✳ 1 ✳··

What creative choice am I navigating right now?

··✳ 2 ✳··

What's one potential path I can follow?

··✳ 3 ✳··

What's a different potential path I can follow?

··✳ 4 ✳··

Which path will I try out first?

Move On Meaningfully

with the

VIII

Eight of Cups

The Eight of Cups challenges you to be brave enough to walk away from things you've loved creating to make space for new creative adventures.

The card stands at the intersection of woe and optimism. It acknowledges that choosing to leave behind one creative dream to seek a new one is not easy, but it can be freeing. When you stop carrying the burden of what could have been, you open up space in your mind and your heart for new potential to take root. You don't just move on—you move forward.

Honoring both the excitement and the difficulty that comes with moving on can be a comfort as you navigate choices and priorities in your creative life. You can move on from a project you once loved with grace and respect, knowing you don't have to carry it as a regret or failure, but rather acknowledging that whatever you built has gotten you this far. Now, it's time to go even further on your own.

Total Eclipse of Creativity

There are some particularly rich symbols in this card.

The eclipse in the sky offers lots to think about. It could prompt you to consider how the things you're clinging to are eclipsing your full creative potential. On the flip side, it might trigger thoughts about how the most important ideas, the ones you need to move forward with, can eclipse the pain of leaving other pursuits behind.

Then there's the asymmetrical structure of the stack of cups in the foreground. On the bottom, four cups stand side by side in a neatly joined line, but on top of them, two cups are balanced next to each other while another stands apart. The image conjures a sense of incompletion. In a creative context, the card can give you permission to leave things unfinished—to move toward the next thing instead of forcing yourself to tie up all the loose ends on the projects and ideas that are no longer working for you.

In the Smith-Waite tarot deck, illustrator Pamela Colman Smith included visual cues to give the central figure of this card certain qualities in common with the Fool of the Major Arcana. You could think of the Eight of Cups as a prequel or sequel to the Fool card. In either case, it's a reminder that your creative journey is full of highs, lows, and everything in between. Some days you feel light, primed, and ready to leap into your next adventure. Other days, taking the next step is hard, but necessary.

Creative Prompts for the Eight of Cups

Write a dialogue between yourself and a creative pursuit you know you're ready to let go of, even if you're struggling to cut the cord. Use this scene to explore how you can let that creative dream down gently, with honor and respect, and how you can give yourself permission to move forward.

Sketch, paint, or photograph a piece inspired by the eclipse in the Eight of Cups. Reflect on where you have experienced creative eclipses in your life, and you can capture that in your art.

Design a memento mori, a reminder that leaving some creative dreams behind to pursue new ones is a critical part of your creative process. This may be an item you display in your workspace, a piece of jewelry, a tattoo design, or something else entirely.

Journal about a time when you let something go and grew from it. Try to remember exactly what it felt like to choose to move on, and think about how you feel about that choice now, having seen the consequences.

The Eight of Cups Spread

Turn to this spread when you need some support as you evaluate your priorities and prepare to let go of some of your darlings.

Shuffle your deck, then flip through until you find the Eight of Cups. Lay the three cards that come after it in your deck out in the pattern that follows. Then, reflect on how each card relates to the question asked.

·· 1 ··

What am I
ready to leave
behind?

2

What's keeping me
from moving on?

·· 3 ··

How can I
honor what
I'm moving on
from?

Take Pride in Your Creative Work

IX

with the Nine of Cups

Elsewhere in the suit of Cups, you've learned about the importance of celebrating and rewarding yourself for your creative achievements. Now, the Nine of Cups offers you a chance to build on that practice of celebrating your creative work by *showing off* your artistic output.

There's a difference between rewarding *yourself* for a job well done and making sure other people know just how talented and creative you are. Your creative work can easily stay a well-kept secret if you celebrate privately. If that's the way you like it, then feel free to keep focusing on celebrating yourself. But if part of your creative vision is to make a living from your art or your creative thinking, it's crucial to show yourself off.

The Nine of Cups captures the attitude of pride you should bring to your work as a creative. In the image, the central figure sits before a showcase of cups, proudly claiming credit for the pristine items laid out on the table. Their crossed arms could suggest smug confidence or discomfort with the spotlight—a contradiction that might ring very true to your own experience of showing your work. You feel that sense of pride in your work deep down, but you may also feel nervous and vulnerable about whether your audience will validate you.

The Nine of Cups is here to back you up with an emphatic yes. Yes, your work is worth your pride. Yes, your work is allowed to take up space. Yes, it's important to put yourself out in the world with confidence and faith that other people will find something meaningful in what you've created.

Be the Advocate for Your Art

This card is here to remind you that you are the greatest advocate for your creative work. If you want people to love what you've made, you have to show them that you love it first. This can be vulnerable, cringey, even scary, especially if you've ever been told by a parent, teacher, or other meaningful person in your life that your work is not valuable. Unlearning that mindset and showing up with confidence and bravado as an artist is the real challenge this card presents.

Pull out the Nine of Cups anytime you feel like you're experiencing resistance around sharing your work with others. Taking strength from the card's bold, confident, unapologetic attitude can help you give yourself permission and encouragement to put your work out there.

Creative Prompts for the Nine of Cups

Design a portfolio that shows off your best creative work and gather loving, appreciative quotes to include alongside your pieces. Quotes may come from clients or buyers, but can absolutely come from friends and family, too.

Create a self-portrait that casts you as the central figure in the Nine of Cups. What are you showing off in the image? How will you display it in your self-portrait to make it obvious that you're proud of what you're presenting?

Write a clever advertisement or jingle that best expresses what makes you great as a creative. Have fun with this—no one has to see or hear it, but remember that the lesson of the card is that people should see your work.

Journal about any memories you have of displaying or showcasing your creative work in the past. Were these negative or positive memories? How do they inform the way you feel when you meditate on the Nine of Cups?

The Nine of Cups Spread

Even the most confident creatives like to be reminded of how great they are.

This spread is designed to help you identify creative achievements you deserve to show off.

Shuffle your deck and pull out nine cards, keeping them face down. Turn over any three you feel most drawn to, and then lay them out in the pattern that follows. Then reflect on how each card relates to the question asked.

··✳ 1 ✳··

What's something I've accomplished in my creative life?

··✳ 2 ✳··

What's something else I've accomplished in my creative life?

··✳ 3 ✳··

What's another creative accomplishment I deserve to be proud of?

Find Creative Paradise

with the

X

Ten of Cups

Many tarot readers see the Ten of Cups as a promise of domestic fulfillment, and it's easy to see why: In this portrait of bliss, a happy family rejoices beneath a rainbow full of sparkling cups. The clear skies, fertile landscape, and dancing children speak to a sense of pleasure, prosperity, even paradise.

If this card comes up for you in a moment when you're experiencing creative bliss, take the time to soak it up, to luxuriate in what you've got going for you in this moment. Reflect on the strategies and happy accidents that got you here; make art from this place of joy; and savor the moment.

But if you find yourself pulling this card during a time where your creative life feels anything but a prosperous, pleasure-filled paradise, know that it still has plenty to say to you in this moment.

Let's first remember that tarot cards are not promises. They're mirrors; they're maps. It's up to you to see yourself, up to you to take in the lay of the land and make your way forward on your own two feet.

Chart Your Own Paradise

The Ten of Cups is here to remind you that paradise can be here, now, and you can appreciate it even while you're navigating hardships in your life. The key lies in the rainbow symbol that dominates the frame of the card.

On first glance, the rainbow is just another sugary sweet element of the card's almost too-good-to-be-true depiction of paradise. But when you start to think about rainbows just a little bit, you can deepen the way the card speaks to you.

Rainbows, of course, are the direct result of rain. And getting caught in the rain—much like getting caught up in creative blocks or dissatisfaction—can weigh you down and ruin your day. The rainbow, then, is a reminder that paradise is earned. That enduring the rain is the secret to appreciating paradise. And that, like rain and rainbows, blocks *and* moments of creative bliss will happen again and again, many times throughout your life.

When the Ten of Cups appears in a reading, it's a reminder that there may be no permanent utopia—not in your creative life, and not in life in general. But, more importantly, it offers comfort: There can be moments of brilliant color as a storm eases off. Allowing yourself to fully experience that moment, rather than trying to make that moment last forever, is its own perfect kind of paradise.

Creative Prompts for the Ten of Cups

Make a piece of visual art inspired by the rainbow in the Ten of Cups. How can you bring something new to this classic symbol in your own, unique style?

Write a poem or essay about a blissful moment on your creative journey.

Redesign this card in a way that illustrates a different kind of paradise, one that doesn't rely on the nuclear family as a symbol. Think about the kind of paradise that makes room for your individual needs and desires, and illustrate it.

Journal about how this moment, right now, the one in which you're putting pen to paper to reflect on, is a kind of paradise in its own right.

The Ten of Cups Spread

Turn to this spread when you need support in appreciating and reveling in the moments of paradise available to you here and now.

Shuffle your deck and then flip through until you find the Ten of Cups. Take the card directly behind it out of your deck, and lay it in the first card position that follows. Then shuffle again, and look for the Ten of Cups in your deck for a second time. Lay the card behind the Ten of Cups next to the first card you laid down. Reflect on how each card relates to the question asked.

·•* 1 *•·

What storm am I currently weathering my way through?

·•* 2 *•·

How can I find paradise now, while I navigate that storm?

Get Playful with the

Page of
Cups

It's crucial to prioritize play in your creative life, because play is the food your imagination thrives on. Play allows ideas to take root—it's how creatives develop original, unique work. Without play, your creative muscles atrophy. You can't make anything without the materials and confidence you generate through having fun.

Unfortunately, modern society doesn't give play the respect it deserves. Many creative people associate their need for fun and novelty with the shame they've been taught to feel around procrastination, mental rest, and nonlinear thinking.

When you grow up being taught that play is a distraction, reintegrating it as an essential ingredient for your creative success can be challenging. The Page of Cups can help you reacquaint yourself with your sense of play, and develop confidence in the importance of creative fun in your life.

Stop Trying to Get Play "Right"

Front and center of the card is our Page, a jaunty figure decked out in flamboyant, colorful clothes. The Page's body language oozes confidence—a willingness to take up space—without edging over into self-importance. That attitude is critical for a healthy sense of playfulness in your creative life. You want to trust yourself to embrace playfulness without putting pressure on yourself to *achieve* or *perform* playfulness.

The delicate balance between embracing playfulness and pressuring yourself to get play "right" is captured through the delightfully weird interplay between the Page and the fish inside the cup.

Finding a fish in your cup is not, on first thought, a welcome or appetizing experience. But you can see, through the Page's body language and the overall mood of the card, that there's no shock, animosity, or even mild distaste in this exchange. Instead, the Page seems to take the appearance of the fish as an amusing development. That's the same attitude you want to take toward play.

By allowing yourself to be open to amusements, flights of fancy, and weird things that you didn't expect to float across your mind, you gain access to a highway to new creative ideas.

When the Page of Cups comes up in a reading, take it as an invitation to tap into your curiosity and delight. And whenever you feel a sense of play is lacking in your creative life, meditate on this card, or use the Page of Cups spread to help you integrate and celebrate creative playfulness more fully.

Creative Prompts for the Page of Cups

Create a 3D work of art inspired by the Page of Cups. What weird, unexpected, imaginative element can you put inside a cup of your own?

Write a short story, script, or poem that is created from a sense of play, instead of an artistic or craft sensibility. What happens when you throw the rule book out and just play on the page?

Make yourself a creative toy box full of objects and prompts that make you feel playful (this book and your tarot deck could go into it!). Keep the toy box accessible, and dive into it at least once a week, just for the sake of getting some creative playtime in.

Journal about the most playful period of your life so far. What nourished your imagination during that time, and how can you incorporate some of the magic from that era into your life now?

The Page of Cups Spread

Creativity is all about turning play into art, but even the most creative minds need a little prompting from time to time.

This spread is here for you anytime you want to connect to your sense of playfulness and prepare for the hurdles you might face while prioritizing play.

Shuffle your deck and choose three cards. Lay them face down in the pattern that follows and turn them over one by one, so you can take in the message of each card one at a time. Then reflect on how each card relates to the question asked.

··✳ 2 ✳··

What challenge might I face while trying to get playful?

··✳ 1 ✳··

What theme or subject can I get playful with?

··✳ 3 ✳··

How can I overcome that challenge and embrace play?

Connect to Your **Creative Core**

with the

Knight of Cups

For tarot readers with a passion for myth, the Knight of Cups seems to nod to the legend of King Arthur and the Holy Grail. In literature and lore, King Arthur's knights go on a quest for the lost Grail, a mythic cup that has come to be associated with knowledge, healing, and incorruptible power. In the legend, the Grail is pure goodness, and the knights who successfully recovered it from its hiding place had to be pure of heart and intention to succeed in their quest.

So, this card can be a prompt to explore your own purest intentions, your most uncorrupted desires, the true core of who you are. The quest to go deep into your own heart is crucial for living a fulfilled life, and it's doubly important for living a fulfilled *creative* life. Because until you understand yourself, your own purest intentions and uncorrupted desires, the ideas you bring into the world will merely be pale imitations of your real creative potential.

Map Out the Goals in Your Creative Quest

When the Knight of Cups comes up in a reading, consider it an invitation to reconnect with the core of who you are and what you want as a creative. It's a sign to simplify, purify, and realign your creative quest to your true desires.

The card may prompt you to explore some deep questions such as these: Does the creative work I'm doing make me feel fulfilled? Are my creative priorities in line with my values? Does my creative life look like I want it to?

You may not like the answers to all the questions, but you will most definitely find wisdom in the process of asking. You'll discover whether you need to course correct or hold fast to the path you're already on.

The most important reminder offered by the Knight of Cups is that your creative journey is your own personal Grail quest.

By setting out to express yourself, to bring your ideas into reality, you're seeking what many before you have searched for: answers, heart, meaning, connection. When you intentionally go after giving these things to yourself, the work you create will naturally propel you along the path to your own Grail.

Remember that to discover the core of who you are as a creative is a quest that never ends, one that will keep offering up answers, heart, and meaning along the way.

Creative Prompts for the Knight of Cups

Draft a creative manifesto that speaks to who you know yourself to be. In ten lines, the manifesto should capture your creative values, your most vital creative dreams, and your personal commitment to living those values and dreams in your life.

Create a soundtrack for your current creative quest. What songs best reflect you and what you want out of your mission?

Produce a short, silent film that follows an artist on a quest. Get creative with how you illustrate what they want and why it matters.

Journal about how your experience with tarot up to now has enriched, informed, and clarified your creative journey.

The Knight of Cups Spread

Connecting to your creative core requires a balancing act of intentionality and open-mindedness. This spread is designed to help you practice both, and to gain clarity on your quest to live a more creative life.

Before you shuffle your deck, consciously choose a card you feel best represents your truest creative desire. Take it out of the deck and lay it in the first position of the following spread. Then shuffle, and draw three more cards to complete the pattern. Reflect on how each card relates to the question asked.

·❊ 1 ❊·

What card do I choose to represent my truest creative desire?

·❊ 2 ❊·

What will I need to overcome on my quest to fulfill my creative desire?

·❊ 3 ❊·

What wisdom will help me along the way?

·❊ 4 ❊·

How will this quest help me grow in my creative life?

Your Own Safe Harbor

with

the

King

of

Cups

The King of Cups feels like coming home after a hard day. There's a sense of calm-amid-a-storm that makes this card both comforting and aspirational: This King can be a safe harbor for you no matter how chaotic the circumstances. It can also challenge you to seek out and create that sense of safety within yourself.

A lot of creative blocks stem from the need for the "right" circumstances in which to create. You tell yourself you'll start your creative business when things at your nine-to-five job settle down, or when your kids start school. You book a writing retreat for three months from now, and plan to write your entire book then. You need to be "in the mood" to paint, or have the perfect charcoal pencil to start sketching. You need to learn how to use the right software before you can create in a new medium. Your personal and professional life are just too stressful for your creative juices to flow.

All of those things may feel true, and it's understandable that you might question your creative skills and priorities when you feel under pressure in other areas of your life. But the King of Cups offers an alternative way of navigating your relationship with creativity.

Let Your Creativity Protect You

Too often, we talk ourselves out of showing up in the world because we believe there's a right time and place to be creative. We convince ourselves that we need to protect our creativity from the chaos in our lives. But if you imagine your creative life as the stable, solid foundation that the King of Cups rests on, you can flip the script. You don't need to protect your creativity from the chaos of the world. You can let your creativity protect you. You can let your creativity be your lighthouse on dark and stormy seas.

By nurturing the belief that creative expression plays a crucial role in keeping you afloat and alive in this world, you can drop the excuses that keep you from making your art.

This card offers a critical comfort: You don't need to fix everything in your life before you dedicate yourself to your creativity. You can look to your creative experience as a balm for the things that feel broken and messy.

When you allow your creativity to play the role of King of Cups in your life, you'll find new ways of navigating the stormy seas around you, and new ways of keeping yourself afloat on your own terms.

Creative Prompts for the King of Cups

Create a visual piece of art that reimagines this card based on your own experience. Illustrate the stormy seas as the things that stress you out and keep you from creating. Create your own version of the King of Cups figure to capture the creative practices that make you feel safe and empowered.

Write a story about an explorer lost at sea. How do they get to safety, and what do they learn along the way?

Craft a piece of jewelry that is infused with the King of Cups themes, and wear it to remind you to be your own safe harbor.

Journal about ways you can establish a sense of creative safety and consistency for yourself amid the chaos of your life. What small rituals might you want to incorporate into your life, or what small space in your home or work can you redesign to feel like a physical manifestation of the King of Cups?

The King of Cups Spread

Building a relationship with your creativity so that your practice is your safe space can be challenging, but it's a crucial mind shift.

To represent the background of chaos in the card, spread your cards out face down in a messy pile on the floor or on your desk. Close your eyes and run your hand over the pile, count to five, and draw the card your hand lands on when you hit five. Reflect on how the card you drew can give you insight into the following question.

·· ✴ 1 ✴ ··

How can I find safety and security through my creative practice right now?

Cherish Your Creations

with
the
Queen
of Cups

The Queen's cup is unlike any other vessel you see in the whole suit of Cups. Until now, every cup in every card has been a uniform shape and style. But this cup breaks the mold, and the Queen adores it for that—you can tell by the way they angle their body and face toward the singular object.

True creative fulfillment is surely something like what's brought to life on the Queen of Cups' face—that awe and delight, that certainty that what you're holding in your hands is the only thing like it in the entire world.

But you may find it difficult to look at your own art the way the Queen looks at this one-of-a-kind cup. Maybe you're afraid it will come off vain. Or maybe someone told you that your creations aren't worth the kind of love the Queen is offering their chalice. Maybe it's just never occurred to you that you're allowed to wholeheartedly adore the things you make.

But you are allowed. No matter what anyone else thinks, or what anyone else might have told you, or might still say. You're allowed to look in wonder on your creations, even if the only person they're beautiful to is you.

Be into Yourself

We live in a world that equates humility with self-deprecation. We learn that in order to be seen as worthy by others, we can't appear too confident about our own worth, lest we come off as self-obsessed.

Cherishing your work and recognizing what makes it special to you is not something you should deny yourself simply because someone else might think you're too into yourself.

BE INTO YOURSELF. Creativity *is about being into yourself.* It's about looking within yourself and offering what you find to the world through your art. If you can't fall in love with what you're making, what does it really matter whether anyone else thinks it's good?

Like all of the Queens in the tarot, the Queen of Cups hands you a direct invitation to own an aspect of yourself and wear it proudly. In this case, you're asked to own the love that keeps you creating. To stop denying yourself the full, beautiful, emotive experience of your creative process. To love what you make like it's your child; to admire your work just exactly as it is.

Creative Prompts for the Queen of Cups

Make a piece of art in the medium of your choice that depicts something that you love as much as the Queen loves the cup in this card. What does it feel like to create from a place of adoration?

Script and film a short video inspired by this card. Who is your Queen, and what form does the cup take? How do the themes of this video speak to the underlying lesson in the card?

Write a love poem for one thing you've created that you truly adore—however far back in your creative life you have to look to find it. The poem should be at least fifteen lines and should recreate the sense of pure admiration you feel when you think about it.

Journal about something you've created that deserves more of your love, for the sheer fact that you made it at all. Write a list of ten reasons you love this piece of work, even if you never shared it with anyone, even if you never want to.

The Queen of Cups Spread

This spread will help you explore ways to cherish, rather than judge, your creative work.

Shuffle your deck, then flip through until you find the Queen of Cups. Lay out the three cards directly behind the Queen in the pattern that follows. Then, reflect on how the cards you drew can offer insight into these questions.

·❋ 1 ❋·

What's one thing I can do to love my creative work more fully right now?

·❋ 2 ❋·

What's one thing holding me back from loving my creative work more fully?

·❋ 3 ❋·

How can I prioritize what I love about my work over what I fear or dislike?

CUPS EXERCISES

Exercise 1

Write a script and film a short movie that casts the Page, Knight, King, and Queen of Cups as the main characters. Who are they to each other, and what do they want from each other? If you need help bringing tension or a goal to the story, draw a Sword or Wand card to indicate what each character might want from the others.

Exercise 2

Lay all fourteen Cups cards out on the table, and choose the three that you find most compelling in this moment. Create a piece of art in the medium of your choice to illustrate an element from each of the three cards you've chosen.

Exercise 3

Look to the Cups to help you solve problems creatively in your work or home life by drawing a Cups card before important conversations. Reflect for a few minutes about how the Cup card gives you insight into the emotional considerations of the conversation. How could this card help you be more empathetic to the person you're speaking to, articulate your emotional needs more clearly, or come up with emotionally satisfying solutions you might not have originally considered?

Exercise 4

Shuffle your deck, then flip through your cards and select the first Cup card and the first Major Arcana card that appear. What feeling do you get by looking at the two cards together? Create a collage that draws out the combined energy of both cards.

The Swords

The Swords' reputation often precedes them: They are the "scary" suit of the tarot, the "dark" cards. There's a sliver of truth to that—if you had to assign a movie genre to the Swords, it would be horror all the way.

Yet, look deeper, and you'll see that despite their spiky appearances, these cards are incredible healers, not least because they challenge you to face your fears—to examine and treat your wounds.

Traditionally, the Swords are the tarot suit that governs the mind. These cards deal with the way you think and the knowledge you put to use. You might imagine the Swords as representations of how your own thinking and bias generate the "scary" quality of the illustrations. Making a study of the Swords means challenging the way you think, addressing biases, and opening your mind to possibilities that feel positive instead of damning.

Being in touch with your fears, and having the presence of mind to reframe the ones that are unhelpful, is one of the most crucial skills you need to master if you want to live a creative life.

Unaddressed fears will keep you from creating. Point blank. If you feel creatively blocked, odds are there's a fear keeping you from exploring the options for moving forward. It could be a tiny fear: *I'm afraid that if I use the wrong color, I'll have to throw this canvas out.* Or it could be a big one: *I'm afraid that if I write this memoir, my family and friends will stop speaking to me.* It could be a practical fear: *I'm afraid that starting this business will undermine my financial security.* Or it could be a deeply personal one: *I'm afraid that people won't enjoy my performance.*

Whatever you're afraid of, the Swords offer you the chance to confront and rethink those fears, opening your mind to new ways of seeing the scary side of your creative journey. They are keys for unlocking your own bravery, so that you can blaze forward on your creative path.

Cut Through Negativity

with the

Ace of Swords

Despite its dark reputation, the suit of Swords opens with optimism. As the first card in the suit, the Ace of Swords captures all the potential and power the Swords have to offer. The crown and laurels placed atop the Sword represent victory. While many of the cards in this suit represent the mindset traps and fears we often think ourselves into, this Ace is a gift: It's the tool you need to gain ultimate victory over your negative, fearful thoughts.

By viewing this card as an antidote to the darkness that follows through the rest of the suit, you can imagine yourself going into your own dark moments and approaching your fears armed with the Ace of Swords' triumphant energy. You've got this.

What Tools Can Help You Confront Your Fears?

The Ace of Swords directs you to cut through the noise of anxious, fearful thought spirals that generate dread, fear, discomfort, or insecurity so that you have a clear path to creative freedom. It promises that when you take action to cut down the negative thought patterns that stand in the way of your creative ambitions, you win.

Think about it: If you cut the cable that was transmitting all your fears, negativity, and insecurities straight into your mind, how much more fun, how much more play, how much more creative abundance might you experience?

When the Ace of Swords comes up for you in a tarot reading, challenge yourself to confront your fears and negative thoughts and consider what tools and resources you need to cut through them.

One powerful tool the Ace of Swords might stand in for is therapy, counseling, or coaching. Having the space and support of another person can help you identify and break through negative thought patterns—effectively cutting through the noise so you can hear and attend to your own needs.

You might also find Ace of Swords energy through journaling, meditation, or, of course, the tarot—a brilliant tool that allows you to practice self-work and creative thinking at the same time. All of these resources can help you follow the card's advice to overcome your fears by cutting through the noise and fog of your insecurities and anxieties.

Creative Prompts for the Ace of Swords

Make a list of the negative thoughts that keep you from actioning your creative ambitions. Fill up a whole page if you need to. Then, fold it up as many times as you can, grab a pair of scissors, and make confetti out of it. Every time you cut, remind yourself that your creativity is so much bigger than your fears.

Design your own version of this card, but transform the sword into a creative tool that helps you cut through the noise of your negative thoughts. It might be a paintbrush, a camera, a pen, a phone, or something more abstract.

Write yourself a letter full of positive affirmations. Seal it in an envelope and keep it somewhere that you can access for when you find yourself overwhelmed by negative thought patterns. When the time is right, open it with a letter opener or butter knife to symbolize the Ace of Swords. (Or just rip it open if you don't have a tool on hand.)

Journal about what you might do, make, or achieve if you weren't weighed down by negative thoughts.

The Ace of Swords Spread

Turn to this spread whenever you need help recognizing what's clouding your vision so that you can cut through and move forward.

Shuffle your deck, then flip through it until you find the Ace of Swords. Split the deck in two from there, draw a card from the top of each pile, and lay them down in the pattern that follows. Reflect on how the cards you draw relate to the prompts in the spread.

⁘ 2 ⁘

How can I cut through the fog and move forward on my creative journey?

⁘ 1 ⁘

What fears are clouding my creative vision?

Uncomplicate Your Overwhelm

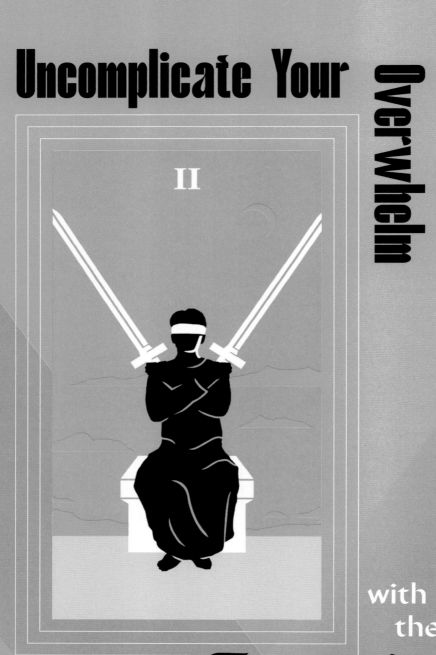

with the

Two of Swords

Traditionally, Two of Swords is a representation of indecision, but there's more to this card than being caught at a crossroads. The Two of Swords is about being completely overwhelmed by your situation, and feeling unable to move forward in any direction at all.

It can be a frustrating card to pull: There's a lot going on in the image and yet, nothing is happening. Creative block, or periods of creative dissatisfaction, can feel like that, like you're too weighed down to engage with your creativity or put any one of your ideas into action.

But looking at the image, you have to wonder: Why won't this figure set down at least one of their swords, remove the blindfold, and get some clarity on the situation?

The image seems to illustrate the "freeze" fear response. Rather than fighting (they have the swords to do it) or fleeing (they could put the swords down, stand up, take the blindfold off, and run), this figure is stuck in a space of complete overwhelm. It's all too much.

This card can validate those moments when you just feel absolutely incapable of moving forward, but it also offers some advice: Remember yourself.

Return to Your Own Depths

The moonlit sea behind the figure is a crucial but often ignored element in this card. In the tarot, water isn't just wet; it's a symbol for the subconscious, for depth, for intuition, and emotional literacy. The fact that it takes up so much space in this image is important, and that the figure has their back to the vast ocean representing their intuitive knowledge is key. This character is not just blind to what's in front of them, but they're also blind to what's within them.

When you recognize the significance of the ocean, you can see the Two of Swords as an invitation to shed your burdens and return to yourself. To step away from the overwhelming pressure to *act*, or to have it all figured out, planned, and ready to go.

Let this card prompt you to refocus your efforts on understanding yourself. Put down your weapons. Free your hands to remove the blindfold. Stand up, turn around, and remember that one of the most important things you can do for your creativity is to engage with your own depths.

You don't have to take action, you don't have to produce work, you just have to dip your toes into the water and connect with yourself.

Creative Prompts for the Two of Swords

Write a story or script about a character who feels stuck as a result of neglecting their own instincts. How will they return to themselves over the course of the story?

Explore movement inspired by this card: Sit in the same posture as the central figure, with your arms crossed over your chest and eyes closed. Take a deep breath in, and, as you exhale, open your eyes and stand up with your legs spread, opening your arms to their full width. Inhale and bring yourself back to sitting. Repeat this a few times, and notice how different the body feels in each posture.

Create a piece of art that depicts what the central figure in this card might see if they took their blindfold off.

Journal about how you stay connected with your own instincts and intuition. How can you prioritize this connection?

The Two of Swords Spread

Use this spread to help you face overwhelm and return to your creative depths so that you can move forward.

Close your eyes and shuffle your deck. When you're ready to draw cards, open your eyes, spread the deck out face down in front of you, and draw four cards. Lay them down in the pattern that follows and then reflect on how the cards you draw relate to the prompts in the spread.

··❋ 1 ❋··
Where is my overwhelm rooted?

··❋ 2 ❋··
What can I set aside to free myself up?

··❋ 3 ❋··
How can I stop and reconnect with my creative depths?

··❋ 4 ❋··
How can I preempt overwhelm in the future?

Let It All Out with the

III

Three of Swords

If you google the Three of Swords (don't), you'll get a swathe of unwelcome keywords: heartbreak, sorrow, humiliation, misfortune.

In a creative context, I like to think of the Three of Swords differently. Yes, it acknowledges and illustrates some tough experiences—an image of a heart stuck through by three swords while rain pours in the background undeniably suggests some very real angst.

But the card is not predictive; it's not designed to prepare you for some future heartbreak. Instead, it holds space for whatever big feeling is already weighing heavy on your heart. It's here to remind you that your job as a creative is to feel that feeling, to create honestly and openly from it, instead of running the other way.

When I look at the swords stuck through the heart, I don't think of stabbing. I think of something slightly less dramatic but maybe a little more distasteful: lancing a boil or a blister. The swords don't pierce the heart aiming to kill, but to release and relieve a buildup of pain.

Following that metaphor, the swords in this image are transformed from murder weapons into instruments of healing; they facilitate the release of buildup in the heart. They offer the chance to let it all out and let it all go.

Pierce Your Protection

Many creative people walk around with metaphorical blisters: aspects of your creative self that are inflamed and scary to touch.

These parts of you might have been rubbed raw by external criticism, internal frustration, or trauma from other areas of your life.

Whatever the reason for the pain you're feeling, you've developed an aversion to touching it, a fear of engaging with it. As long as that aversion and fear are stronger than your curiosity and self-compassion, you may feel creatively blocked, emotionally exhausted, and generally unsatisfied.

When the Three of Swords comes up for you, it's time to lance your creative blisters. Pierce through the protective barrier you've put between yourself and the world and let what's inside you out. Express it through your creative pursuits, by creating art about it, or simply by being honest with your audience about what you've been through.

Creative Prompts for the Three of Swords

Create your own version of this card using any visual medium that feels right to you: photography, collage, paint, sculpture, film. Aim to explore, engage with, and articulate your sore spots with curiosity and compassion.

Experiment with automatic writing or painting. This means making without thinking, just allowing whatever comes out to manifest. It can be a frustrating task for beginners, but it's OK to repeat the lines "I don't know what to write" until something else takes hold, or to paint the same pattern over and over until you're inspired. As long as something is coming out of you, even if it feels boring, you're doing it right. Keep this practice up for a week and see what happens.

Write a haiku about a difficult feeling you're having trouble engaging with. Because the haiku style is short and formulaic, it can be a good way to test the waters. Use this prompt to help you start your haiku: "I'm scared to say this, but here it is:"

Journal about the things that keep you from expressing yourself fully. What fears, old wounds, and aversions are standing in the way of you showing up to your creative pursuits in the most authentic, honest, vulnerable, open way you can?

The Three of Swords Spread

This spread is here to support you in letting the scary stuff out. When pulling cards in this spread, make sure you're in an environment that feels safe for you, and that you've put aside time to process what comes through.

When you're ready to pull cards, shuffle your deck and take a deep breath in. Release that breath with an audible sigh, and draw a card from the deck. Repeat this until you've drawn all three cards and placed them in the pattern that follows. Then, reflect on what the cards are communicating through the spread.

··✳ 1 ✳··

What am I avoiding expressing through my creative work?

··✳ 2 ✳··

What fear is perpetuating that avoidance?

··✳ 3 ✳··

How can I start to express my full experience?

Give Yourself Mental Space

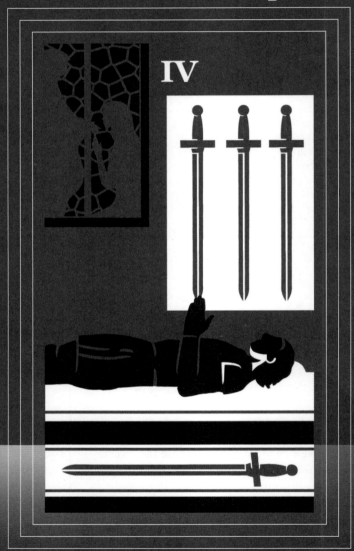

with
the
Four of Swords

Most creative people think and move fast. We're impulsive, we're responsive, we're dynamic. These qualities often help us come up with exciting new solutions or highly resonant and deeply felt artistic expressions. But these qualities can also be exhausting, and they don't allow much time or space for rest or for processing.

Creativity needs time to percolate. Ideas need quiet space to develop, and our experiences need to be reflected on and processed before we can create meaningfully in response to them. But giving ourselves that time can be scary, and we often judge ourselves harshly for needing it.

The Four of Swords can be your permission slip to take your time, and a reminder that you deserve to process information, experiences, and emotions so that you can transform it all into creative fuel.

You may not always be able to drop everything and delve deep into a self-care practice, but this card defends taking mental space not just as an emotional ideal but also as a physical and mental necessity.

It's not a restful card, but it endorses rest anyway. When it appears, it's time to press pause even when logic says you just have to grit your teeth and stick something out. That pause won't fix everything—the swords hanging over your head are still going to be there when your wake up. But giving yourself a moment of peace, security, and retreat when you need it is critical for sustaining yourself through hard stuff.

Realistic Retreat

Several cards within the tarot promote rest and space to think (see the Star, the Hanged One, and the Two and Three of Wands), but the Four of Swords is by far the most pragmatic and functional.

In this card, we don't get a romanticized illustration of rest but a more realistic picture: A soldier has retreated from the battlefield for a nap in a sanctuary.[2] This knight doesn't have time to strip their armor or create a comfortable, cushioned space to sleep. Above them, three swords hanging on the wall give the impression that the sleeping knight is about to be stabbed through. And still, they take this precious moment to recharge so they can dive back into battle.

For many busy, multi-hyphenate creatives, this is reality: You have to steal moments of sanctuary in between battle zones. It doesn't always feel fully refreshing, and it's tempting to skip right over that processing time and space to just power through to the end. But working that way is unsustainable; you need mental space, even if it's in microdoses.

The Four of Swords can support you in taking a time-out whenever you need it rather than whenever it's convenient.

---

2. While A. E. Waite initially imagined this figure as an effigy in a tomb, modern tarot expert Rachel Pollack popularized a softer view of this illustration: the sleeping knight.

Creative Prompts for the Four of Swords

Curate a "sanctuary" playlist that you can put on anytime you need to zone out and be with your thoughts for a few minutes.

Write a silent film about a soldier who finds a moment of rest between battles.

Design a collage inspired by the stained glass window that sits above the sleeping knight. How can you weave the themes present in this card into your art?

Journal about what helps you give yourself mental space to process information, experiences, and emotions.

The Four of Swords Spread

To use this spread, you're going to grant yourself a short moment of rest and retreat by intentionally choosing a card that makes you feel at peace.

Rather than shuffling your deck and drawing cards blind, leaf through the deck, taking each card in, giving yourself a beat to inhale and exhale one deep breath while looking at each image. Choose one card out of the deck that gives you a sense of peace, and sit with it a moment longer. Then carry it with you as the day goes on, pulling it out anytime you need a minute to rest and reset.

·•❋ 1 ❋•·

Which tarot card makes me feel most at peace right now?

Challenge Your Ego

with the

V

Five of Swords

If this card makes you feel on edge, you're not alone. I'm convinced that the Five of Swords was destined by design to call us out.

But don't let its choppy skies and sharp edges keep you from exploring its wisdom. While the Five of Swords is not here to play nice, getting creative with it can be enlightening.

I think tarot cards where multiple characters are present are so creatively gratifying to work with. They offer you the space to imagine which figure you feel drawn to or most able to relate to. The Five of Swords is a perfect example: Depending on which person in the scene most closely reflects how you're feeling, your work with the card will look different.

How Do You See Yourself?

If you see yourself in the central figure in the foreground of the image, then you may be feeling smug about a recent creative success. The card is not necessarily saying you don't deserve to enjoy your win, but it may be inviting you to think about how your actions to get to this point might have been shortsighted. If you burned bridges to get where you are now, or you sacrificed your own safety or comfort, your success may be short-lived or come with unexpected consequences.

If you see yourself in either of the other figures, with their backs turned as they grieve a battle lost, you might be experiencing some sort of disappointment or professional envy. The central figure may stand in as a proxy for someone you resent—a fellow creative, or a gatekeeper in your industry who you feel has kept you from meeting a creative goal. It might also stand in for something you feel is blocking you from achieving your creative ambitions—your own health or financial circumstances, for example.

Whichever element of the scene hits closest to home for you, there's an inherent warning against assuming you know the final outcome of the game. And there's an even sharper challenge to confront your ego. Whether you see yourself as a winner or a loser, the Five of Swords invites you to investigate the price of unchecked ambition and the consequences of entitlement.

When it comes up in a reading, ask yourself: Am I feeling like I have more right to creative success than others, or that I'm a helpless victim? How is my ego or sense of entitlement keeping me from making valuable connections that can help me find creative success and satisfaction in the long run?

Creative Prompts for the Five of Swords

Use the visual elements of this card, like the choppy clouds and windy air, to create a piece of art that captures the same threatening, moody tone that's evident in the card.

Script a dialogue between the three characters in this card. Set it several years in the future, and examine how the outcome of this day affected each of them differently.

Create a comic strip or graphic narrative that examines this scene—and the before and after—for each of the three figures in the card.

Journal about a time you felt entitled to something in your creative life. Was that sense of entitlement helpful? Explore the alternative approaches to achieving a creative goal, without feeling entitled to a win.

The Five of Swords Spread

This spread can prompt you to gently challenge your ego and your perceptions of your wins and losses.

Shuffle your deck and flip through until you find the Five of Swords. Draw out the four cards behind the Five of Swords and lay them out in the pattern that follows. Then, reflect on how the cards you draw relate to the prompts in the spread.

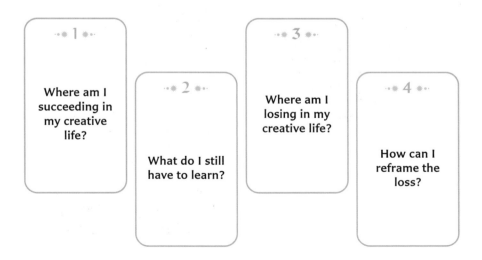

··❊ 1 ❊··
Where am I succeeding in my creative life?

··❊ 2 ❊··
What do I still have to learn?

··❊ 3 ❊··
Where am I losing in my creative life?

··❊ 4 ❊··
How can I reframe the loss?

Make Peace with Your Past

Your Past

VI

with the **Six of Swords**

The Six of Swords is about reckoning with where you've come from, so that you can fully embrace where you're going.

The figures in this card are on the move, determined to get somewhere better than where they left. But the muted colors and the way their backs are to the viewer—not to mention the ominous swords stabbed through the boat—temper the card's optimism, making room for the growing pains that accompany progress.

Moving forward can often mean abandoning unfinished projects or pursuits you deemed "unsuccessful"; to move ahead, you have to make peace with what you're leaving behind, even if you'd rather forget it entirely.

Accept Your Failings, Your Mistakes, Your Regrets

The Six of Swords calls you to reflect on where you're at on your creative journey, in terms of both where you want to go and what's brought you to this point.

Sometimes, looking back at what you're walking away from can be painful. It takes courage and resilience to see the lessons your past has taught you, to get real about what you're leaving behind, and to examine what expectations you have about where you're going.

The swords stabbed through the boat represent the painful experiences, the fears, the failures, the negativity you're carrying with you as you move into a new venture. They're inconvenient—notice how they obscure the passengers' vision, not to mention the fact that they've probably put holes in the boat. But like it or not, the swords are here, and they have to be acknowledged. Plus, they're the only thing plugging the holes they've made. You have to find a way to see past them while making use of them.

When you draw this card, feel encouraged to accept your failings, your mistakes, your regrets, and make use of what you've learned from them. This is the only way to move forward so you can find new hope on the shoreline ahead and become a wiser, more creative version of yourself.

Creative Prompts for the Six of Swords

Hold a funeral for a creative project that you decided to move on from. Say some kind words about it and about who you were as a creative during the time you were working on it. Let this small act bring you some closure, so you can let go of any guilt that's holding you back from new creative pursuits.

Write an essay or film a vlog about a difficult moment in your past that you nonetheless don't regret. Share what you've learned as a result of that experience and how you came to accept what happened and move forward.

Design your own version of this card. Consider using photos from your own archive to represent your past and explore how it carried you to where you are now.

Journal about what you see when you look at the Six of Swords. Where does it breed optimism in you, and what elements of the card make you feel melancholy? What moments in your own life does the card remind you of?

The Six of Swords Spread

Turn to this spread anytime you feel like your relationship to the past is keeping you from moving forward with new creative pursuits.

Shuffle your deck and take six deep breaths. Draw four cards from the top of the deck and lay them out in the pattern that follows. Then, reflect on how the cards you draw relate to the prompts in the spread.

··✳ 1 ✳··

What am I ready to move on from in my creative life?

··✳ 2 ✳··

What's holding me back from moving beyond it?

··✳ 3 ✳··

How can I make peace with my past and move forward?

··✳ 4 ✳··

What can I gain by making peace with my past?

Confront Your Assumptions with the VII

Seven of Swords

The Seven of Swords has a reputation problem. Traditionally, it represents betrayal and cowardice.

The image does have a sly quality; our main character could be a military deserter or spy. While a battle rages in the background, they are running away from an encampment, a handful of swords in their arms. It looks like they're sabotaging or betraying their peers by skipping the fight and raiding the weapons tent on their way out.

But the card raises some questions:

Who says they're not bringing the extra weapons to the battlefield, to give their side an edge? Maybe this isn't a betrayal at all, but a cunning act of bravery.

Or what if they've realized their side is fighting for the wrong thing, and they're righting a wrong?

Maybe they're a longtime objector, engaged in an anti-war protest.

The interesting thing about this card is that the context hugely affects how it's interpreted, maybe more so than any other card in the tarot. The *why* behind the action matters, and that's the true lesson this card can teach you.

Check Your Assumptions at the Door

The Seven of Swords works best as a prompt to challenge your assumptions.

Assuming curbs curiosity, empathy, imagination—the most crucial building blocks of creativity. So, it makes sense that one of the most important things you can do to bolster and nurture your creative practice is to check your assumptions at the door. Leave room for thoughtful interpretations of your own creative work, and practice approaching others' creative work with an open, curious mind.

When the Seven of Swords comes up for you, investigate your assumptions about your own work, your critics, or your audience. Are you jumping to conclusions about how people will react to work you're afraid to put out in the world, or are you inventing a narrative about why people are engaging with your work in a certain way (or not engaging at all)?

By challenging your own assumptions about how other people see your work, you can open up dialogue that benefits everyone. When you come to the drawing board with fewer assumptions, you're more likely to ask interesting questions and find creatively satisfying directions for your art.

Creative Prompts for the Seven of Swords

Write a short story or script that offers three different plots to explain why the figure in the card is running with swords in their hands.

Host a live Q+A or conduct a survey with the key audience for your creative work. Leave your assumptions at the door, and focus on curiosity. What do you want to know about them? What do they like about you? What are they looking for from your work? If doing this in a group feels overwhelming, try taking a potential client or customer out for a casual coffee to get to know them on a one-to-one basis.

Make a list of all the assumptions you have about what people might think of your current creative project. Burn the list and release the pressure of those unfounded conclusions so that you can return to what matters: making something you care about.

Journal about a time you made assumptions or someone made an assumption about you. How did those assumptions affect your relationship, and what do you wish that you, or they, had done differently?

The Seven of Swords Spread

This Seven of Swords spread is designed to help you directly confront the assumptions you make and the ones you're subjected to in your creative life.

Flip through your deck and remove the Seven of Swords, then shuffle while meditating on this card. When you're ready, draw three cards from the deck and lay them out in the spread that follows. Then, reflect on how the cards you draw relate to the prompts in the spread.

··✳ 1 ✳··

How can I challenge my assumptions about myself and my creative work right now?

··✳ 2 ✳··

How can I challenge other people's assumptions about me and my creative work?

··✳ 3 ✳··

How can I challenge my assumptions about other people or experiences in my creative life?

Set Your Creativity Free

with the

VIII

Eight of Swords

If you're looking at the illustration of the Eight of Swords and thinking "no thank you, next please," I get it. The initial impact of the illustration—a figure bound, blindfolded, caged in by swords—is far from encouraging.

But, as usual, the tarot has a few tricks up its sleeve.

What you see at first glance *is* pretty dire, but notice that the figure is not fully closed in, and their feet are not bound. While the blindfold will definitely make it more difficult, nothing's actually stopping the central character in the card from walking out of the incomplete cage of swords. They could even back into the swords surrounding them and use the blade to cut away the bindings on their arms.

The overarching message of the card: You're not as trapped as you think you are.

Creative people are usually very good at thinking ourselves out of tight spots. Creative problem-solving is one of the most sought-after skills on the job market—every team wants someone who can find the loophole in the kind of mess depicted in the Eight of Swords.

But creative people are also very good at convincing ourselves that things are worse than they are. Our overactive imaginations can't help it (see the Ten of Swords for more on that). So when the Eight of Swords comes up for you, it can act as a reminder that whatever mess you're in is reparable; you are more than capable of getting yourself out of any bind, even if everything seems doomed. It's a permission slip to test the boundaries of the situation you're in until you find your way out.

Face the Mess You're In

The Eight of Swords has some significant similarities with a few other cards in the deck: namely, the Two of Swords and the Devil. All three of these cards depict people at a standstill, seemingly incapacitated, when they actually do have the recourse to take action to free themselves.

The dark elements of these cards (particularly in the Eight of Swords and the Devil) acknowledge that it won't be easy to break free, but promise that it *is* possible. These cards all prompt you to rethink your situation and find a way to free yourself, whether that's from self-sabotage (the Devil), overwhelm (the Two of Swords), or any other kind of unexpected and unwelcome mess you find yourself in (the Eight of Swords' cage can represent any number of apparent traps).

So don't cringe away from the violent imagery in the Eight of Swords; instead, face it head-on and ask yourself: How can my creativity free me from the mess I'm in?

Creative Prompts for the Eight of Swords

Paint or doodle an abstract piece of art while blindfolded (or in the dark). Do this to prove you can make something, no matter how good or bad, even when conditions are far from ideal. Any visually impaired readers might try a similar experiment by using your nondominant hand or otherwise barring your access to an ideal creative environment.

Create a collage that combines imagery from the Eight of Swords, the Two of Swords, and the Devil.

Write a poem in eight lines, inspired by a moment in your life that this card reminds you of.

Journal about an aspect of your life right now that is giving Eight of Swords energy. Explore, through the journaling exercise, what recourse you still have to walk away, even if it's almost impossible to fathom.

The Eight of Swords Spread

Whenever you feel yourself trapped by unhelpful thought patterns, turn to this spread to help you consider how you can step out of those traps.

Shuffle your deck, then flip through until you find the Eight of Swords. Pull the card just before it and the card just after it, and lay them out in the spread that follows. Then, reflect on how the cards you draw relate to the prompts in the spread.

··❋ 1 ❋··

Where am I feeling creatively trapped right now?

··❋ 2 ❋··

What can I do to free myself?

Acknowledge Your Anxieties

with the 𝕹ine of 𝕾words

You know that moment when you wake up from a nightmare, your heart still pounding, and your forehead slick with sweat? That unholy in-between feeling of not knowing whether what you just experienced was real or a dream?

That's the feeling the Nine of Swords asks you to confront.

The classic illustration for this card is a dreamer waking from a nightmare, left to reckon with what's real and what's imagined. It's about the anxieties that chase us from our nightmares into our waking hours. The Nine of Swords' advice? Deal with what's plaguing you before it takes over your life.

Anxiety is a gnarly beast, and everyone's approach to managing it looks different. If you struggle with chronic stress and worry— if this card feels all too real for the majority of your daily life—consider this an invitation to seek out the support of a mental health professional or other treatment plans. While tarot can be a brilliant addition to your mental health tool kit, it's important to ensure that you're taking larger steps toward your own care and well-being.

But if you're experiencing more targeted stress related to your creative pursuits, this card can help you acknowledge and accept the discomfort that sometimes comes with living a creative life.

Don't Kill Your Creativity with Fear

Some element of fear is inherent in the creative journey. It's frightening to put yourself out there. If you sometimes wake up in a cold sweat after dreaming that you proposed an idea at work only to be mocked, that no one showed up to your event, or that you failed art class, you're in good company.

I can confess to experiencing many bouts of acute anxiety about this book. What if you don't like it? What if *I* don't like it? But, if I had let myself stay stuck in the Nine of Swords worry cycle, if I'd let my fear talk me out of writing, we wouldn't be here right now. So instead, as I write this, I have to admit that I'm afraid, but that most of my fear comes from my own imagination. I know I can move forward, even with anxiety in my back pocket.

Take the appearance of the Nine of Swords as an opportunity to confront whatever stressors are plaguing your creative life. Size them up. Tell them you see them. But refuse to let them ruin you, because the worst nightmare you could bring to life is the one where you kill your creativity with your fear.

Creative Prompts for the Nine of Swords

Create a work of art that contrasts a good dream with a nightmare; use the same basic elements in both. For example, if your nightmare features a storm, how can you cast a storm in a positive light through the good dream?

Make a list of nine fears that hold you back from creating. Then rewrite these fears as if they were challenges you want to accept.

Write a short story about a character who decides to overcome their greatest fear. What do they do, and how does it change them?

Journal about someone you know who manages their fears, anxieties, and stresses well. What qualities do you see in them that you admire?

The Nine of Swords Spread

Use this spread to help you recognize and hold space for the worries you face in your creative life, then take its advice on how you can move forward even when experiencing creative anxiety and fear.

Close your eyes and shuffle your deck. When you're ready, open your eyes, spread your cards out on the table face down, and choose three cards to lay out in the spread that follows. Reflect on how the cards you draw relate to the prompts in the spread.

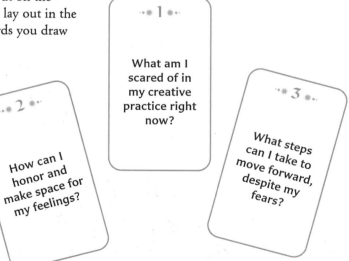

··✳ 1 ✳··
What am I scared of in my creative practice right now?

··✳ 2 ✳··
How can I honor and make space for my feelings?

··✳ 3 ✳··
What steps can I take to move forward, despite my fears?

Quit Catastrophizing

X

with the

Ten of Swords

There's something validating about drawing the Ten of Swords on a bad day—who doesn't love the confirmation that a shitty experience is indeed shitty, and you are allowed to wallow in it?

But it can be deeply troubling to encounter this card when you thought things were going just fine. Your brain might start to worry about all the things that *could* go wrong. You might start inventing every sort of dramatic worst-case scenario.

This penchant for inventing, and fixating on, the worst possible outcome is called "catastrophizing."

Catastrophizing, as it happens, is a highly creative act, and creative people are really good at it. Sometimes that pays off: Much of a novelist's job is coming up with the worst possible things that could happen to their characters. Marketers need to be able to imagine the different problems faced by their target audience and position whatever they're selling as a solution.

While courting catastrophic possibilities can be a skill, constantly expecting the worst can be detrimental for your creative confidence. Too many artists never share their work out of fear that *everyone* will *hate* it. Too many would-be innovators stick to the status quo because they're afraid radical ideas might get them fired or mocked. Too many creatives turn the nasty side of their imaginations on their own lives. This card can be the wake-up call you need to get out of your own head.

Nobody Gets to Defeat You . . . Except You

You might recall another card in the tarot that explores what it means to face your worst-case scenario: the Tower. The two cards do share some DNA: dark, dramatic skies; violence; the initial "oh no" that hits when you draw the card. But there are some marked differences, too.

The Tower depicts a split second; it captures and acknowledges that moment when your world comes crashing down. But it also promises that this rock-bottom experience is temporary: A flash of lightning may raze what you've built, but it ultimately leaves you with a new foundation to build from.

Meanwhile, the Ten of Swords stays stuck in its worst-case scenario. It wallows. It doesn't just take one sword to the back—it takes ten. It's defeated. But *you* don't have to be.

Nobody gets to defeat you except you. Nobody gets to ruin your creative experience except you. Let this card be the tough love reminder that you can rise from the ashes and keep going toward the light of your own creativity.

Creative Prompts for the Ten of Swords

Write a story where your worst-case creative scenario happens to someone else. How does the character react to the experience, and what does it teach you about your own fears?

Create something that really leans into the drama of the Ten of Swords. Maybe it's a soap opera or horror script, a bold, violent painting, or a song that captures the dark drama of the card . . . the only rule is to let yourself wallow in this card's energy for your creative gain.

Sketch out a comic strip that explains how the central figure in this card came to find themselves in this dire position.

Journal about the similarities and differences between the Ten of Swords and the Tower cards. What can these cards teach you about dealing with bad days in your creative life?

The Ten of Swords Spread

Whenever you feel yourself overtaken by a sense of doom and dread in your creative life, turn to this spread to help you reflect on and reframe what you're dealing with.

Spread your cards face down on the table in front of you, mixing them around with your hands. Then pick four cards and lay them out in the spread that follows. Reflect on how the cards you draw relate to the prompts in the spread.

·❋ 1 ❋·

What am I catastrophizing about in my creative life?

·❋ 2 ❋·

How is wallowing in the worst-case scenario holding me back from creative satisfaction?

·❋ 3 ❋·

How can I reframe my fear?

·❋ 4 ❋·

What step can I take to rise out of this rock-bottom feeling?

with
the
Page of
Swords

The Page of Swords is by far the most endearing Swords card (not a hard category to sweep—this suit isn't exactly going for cute and cuddly). It's one of the most generous cards in terms of the advice and grace it has to offer. Among the Swords, the Page can be your breath of fresh air; it's the encouraging sidekick you need to make it through Swords.

Unlike some of the Sword cards that have come before, the wind that creates movement in this card is counterbalanced by more soothing elements: The clouds look fluffy and soft, and a flock of birds wheels through the blue sky overhead.

This Page is a novice warrior, still finding their footing, still learning to wield their sword. They're keen to grow into the knowledge the Swords have to offer, to carve their own path and come out the other side of this suit tougher and more aware of how their fears and pain points affect the way they think and the way they create.

They don't yet know what they don't know, and they're OK with that. They are willing to try, to practice, to get better as they get comfortable with the terrain, the tools they have to work with, and the strengths they'll discover in themselves along the way.

You Don't Have to Be an Expert

Think of this Page as a symbol for embracing a beginners' mindset. It's a card about releasing yourself from expectation around how much knowledge, expertise, skill, talent, and originality you think you need to approach a creative project or pursuit. This card's motto is, "Here I am, as I am, learning as I go."

This willingness to feel a bit foolish, to accept that the early stages of a project—and sometimes the later ones, too—may feel awkward, like the ground is shifting beneath your feet, but it's crucial for living a creative life.

When you're willing to feel like a beginner —even though your mind is telling you that in order to succeed, you should feel like an expert—that's when your creativity is most willing to come out to play.

So when the Page of Swords appears, brace yourself: The way ahead is thorny and you may have no idea what you're doing, but you can give it your best shot anyway.

Creative Prompts for the Page of Swords

Write a story or short film about a character who finds their own Page of Swords energy.

Try a creative discipline you've never worked with before. Experiment with painting, makeup, poetry, coding, sculpture, textile work . . . anything you can come to as a true beginner.

Write an essay or record a vlog about a time you had the courage to step into a new skill and embrace your beginner's mindset. How did that attitude open you up to valuable new experiences?

Journal about how a beginner's mindset can help you bring fresh perspective to a current challenge in your life. How can you accept that you don't need to have the answers, and how can coming to this issue as a beginner help you try new ways of solving it?

The Page of Swords Spread

Use this spread to explore how approaching your creative work with a beginner's mindset can enrich your experience.

Shuffle your deck and take a deep breath, then draw three cards from the top of the deck and lay them out in the spread that follows. Reflect on how the cards you draw relate to the prompts in the spread.

··✳ 1 ✳··

What creative experience do I need to approach as a beginner?

··✳ 2 ✳··

What can I learn through this experience?

··✳ 3 ✳··

How can approaching this experience as a beginner enrich my creativity?

Just Go for It

with the
Knight of Swords

The Swords are the suit of the mind; they give us the power to sharpen our thoughts into clear intentions, rethink the mindsets that are poking holes in our confidence, and cut through our noisy brains to take back the power of our thoughts.

But sometimes, especially in your creative life, you've got to put all your thoughts aside and just do the thing. That's where the Knight of Swords comes rushing in.

This Knight arrives when it's time to quit thinking and start acting. It's a card of pursuit, not reflection or adjustment.

The Knight of Swords challenges you to stop imagining how something might work and instead start testing your ideas in the real world.

Want to start a business? The Knight says pitch potential clients or offer your services or products to friends and family to get feedback.

Want to write a book? The Knight says stop imagining it in your head and put pen to paper.

Want to get a new job? The Knight says send out an application today.

Turn One Thought into One Action

Sometimes, the just-do-it vibes of the Knight of Swords can be difficult to come by, especially if you feel burned out, are under pressure from other areas of your life, or experience challenges with your executive function. If any of these rings true for you, drawing the Knight of Swords may feel like a slap in the face, in which case, maybe it's worth considering that the thing you need to just do most is . . . stop.

If you do have some energy in the tank and you want to try working with the Knight of Swords energy in your creative life, the good news is that it doesn't have to be an all-or-nothing card. When the Knight of Swords shows up, it doesn't mean you have to do everything. It only means you have to do *something*. Anything. Turn one thought into one action, instead of turning all your thoughts over and over in your mind.

If you've drawn the Knight of Swords, or you want to work with what it has to offer you in a creative context, think about the simplest creative action you can take right this moment. Sketch a doodle. Write a haiku. Snap a photo of the view out your window. Call a creative partner or someone who gets you. Hop in the shower and belt out your favorite song, or throw your go-to mix on the speaker and dance it out.

"Going for it" doesn't have to mean getting it all done. It just means starting the charge and seeing how far you get with whatever energy you have.

Creative Prompts for the Knight of Swords

Start a project you've been avoiding or overthinking. Right now. This second. You don't have to commit all day to it, just take one action that gets it 0.01 percent closer to the finish line than it was before you read this prompt.

Pick up a pen and draw the first thing you see. Don't think about it— just sketch it out. What does it feel like to bring this sense of immediate observation to your creative process?

Write a film script about a character in a Knight of Swords moment. What are they charging forward into, and what positive consequences will they experience as a result?

Journal about how overthinking and procrastinating have set you back in your creative process. Explore how the "just do it" attitude of the Knight of Swords can help you move forward.

The Knight of Swords Spread

This spread is all about doing, not thinking; it's designed to be as simple as possible, and uses only one card. Turn to it anytime you're feeling stuck, frustrated, or unsure how to move forward.

Take one big breath, shuffle your deck, split it into two piles, and choose a card off the top of whichever pile you feel most drawn to. Then take an action that aligns with the advice of the card.

··❋ 1 ❋··

What single action can I take now to make something happen in my creative life?

Assert Creative Authority

with the
King of Swords

As a creative, you're probably familiar with the phrase "creativity is subjective."

But we live in a world where creative success is increasingly judged against an objective rubric of KPIs (key performance indicators, like sales, views, or reviews). This outcome-obsessed culture doesn't make the subjective nature of creativity any less real, but it undeniably impacts how you perceive the value of your creativity, and it can often result in a fear of making the "wrong" creative decisions.

A fear of being "wrong" in your creative life can lead to blocks and missed opportunities. While you agonize over which "right" decisions will lead to results, you miss out on important chances to hone your craft and opportunities to commune with and enjoy your creativity. The subjective nature of your creative experience can get lost in the objective demands placed on it.

It's easy to feel jaded as a result of this objectification of creativity. If you've gotten wrapped up in tracking the quantifiables instead of prioritizing your unique process, you might feel that your creativity is failing you, or that you never really had it in the first place (both false, for the record!).

In these moments of doubt, the King of Swords can step in and help you rediscover your own internal rubric for creative success and satisfaction. When you develop your discernment and trust your own judgment, you can re-prioritize your unique creative journey, instead of bowing to a will that's not your own.

Reclaim Your Creative Autonomy

Since the Swords are the suit of the mind and the intellect, they also represent your discernment, your ability to make the right decisions for yourself and stand by them.

The King of Swords is a mascot for being your own authority, for trusting your own discernment, for believing that you're more than capable of making the right decisions for yourself. When the King of Swords appears, see the card as a call to trust your own judgment to define your own success, and to live your creative life by your own rules and standards.

Prompts for the King of Swords

Invent your own creative KPIs, but instead of focusing on things like words written, items sold, or followers gained, try developing a rubric for creative success that focuses more on process than outcome. Set a goal for time spent daydreaming about an idea, or the number of times you've celebrated your progress and skill.

Design a poster or an object you can keep near your desk or in your creative space that will remind you there are no hard-and-fast rules for creativity—you get to make up your own.

Make something that you always held back from making because you were afraid of doing it wrong. Give yourself permission to do it badly, and see what happens.

Journal about what having authority over your own creative life means for you. How much do you already trust your own judgment and where would you like to improve in that area?

The King of Swords Spread

Turn to this spread to help you reclaim your creative authority and autonomy whenever you feel yourself getting wrapped up in external demands placed on your work.

First, pick a number between one and ten. Shuffle your deck that many times and then flip through the cards until you find the King of Swords. Pull the next three cards after the King of Swords and lay them out in the spread that follows. Then reflect on how the cards you draw relate to the prompts in the spread.

·❋ 1 ❋·

What's holding me back from asserting my own creative authority?

·❋ 2 ❋·

How can I reconnect to my own inner sense of what creative success and satisfaction look like for me?

·❋ 3 ❋·

How can reasserting authority in my creative life benefit me?

Rise Above Your Fears

with the Queen of Swords

The Queen of Swords is a portrait of stoicism, a virtue popularized by ancient Greek and Roman philosophers.

The Stoics believed that embracing hardships and seeing difficulties as opportunities to become stronger and more resilient was the work of life. They strived to live humbly, thoughtfully, and wisely. But their modest lifestyles didn't turn the Stoics into hermits—instead, many of them became leaders and teachers. You're probably passingly familiar with the wisdom of the Roman emperor Marcus Aurelius and the statesman Seneca.

These thinkers and their peers found wisdom through the trials of living—they never shied away from their fears and pain, but they never gave in to them either. The Queen of Swords card shares these values and can be a beacon of resilience and stoicism in your creative life. Let the Queen of Swords be your patron saint of moving through your fears, rising above them, and coming out the other side wiser and better equipped to forge ahead on your creative path.

Free Yourself from Fear

You can see in the way the Queen holds themself, in the way their sword rises above the clouds, and in the serious expression on their face that this is not a Queen who luxuriates. This is a Queen who survives. They lead from experience. This Queen knows pain and fear, but also knows the power of overcoming the worst.

In her illustration for this card, Pamela Colman Smith added a crucial detail that we must imagine here: a frayed binding tied around the Queen's left wrist. This symbol is significant because the Swords is a suit deeply preoccupied with bondage—cards like the Two and the Eight of Swords use blindfolds and bonds to represent the things that hold us back, or our fear of the unknown. But, of course, through the entire suit you have the sharp-edged tool you need to cut through those bonds. And in this card, you can see that the Queen of Swords has done exactly that.

This Queen has used their sword—a metaphor for thought process, wisdom, knowledge—to cut through their fears and hang-ups to take their rightful place, presiding over the court of their mind.

This is a card that symbolizes the triumph over your worst moments, your biggest fears. It captures the bravery and stoicism you need to face the hard parts of your creative life and move beyond them, so you can see clearly, beyond the clouds, to the creative future you want and deserve.

Creative Prompts for the Queen of Swords

Create a work of art or write a story that imagines how the Queen of Swords came to be the Queen of Swords. What trials did they face, what traps did they encounter, and how did those experiences transform the Queen into the leader they are now?

Write a song or poem about what you have in common with the Queen of Swords.

Play with the motif of wings. In this card, a bird soars in the clear sky over the Queen's head, and many other versions of the card feature butterfly imagery. What does this card tell you about taking flight, and how can you express that meaning through your art?

Journal about an experience in your life that took bravery and stoicism to confront. How has the moment changed you?

The Queen of Swords Spread

Sometimes we can get lost in the weeds of what's hard and fail to notice how we're evolving for the better. Use this spread to help you reflect on what you've risen above and how you're still rising in your creative life.

Start by shuffling your deck and drawing one card to put in the first position of the spread, then shuffle again and draw a card to put in the second position of the spread, then shuffle a final time and draw a card for the third position of the spread. Reflect on how the cards you draw relate to the prompts in the spread.

··✳ 3 ✳··

What creative opportunities will help me continue to evolve?

··✳ 1 ✳··

How have my past experiences led me to where I am?

··✳ 2 ✳··

Where is my mindset still evolving?

SWORDS EXERCISES

Exercise 1

When you're feeling creatively blocked, separate your deck into two piles: the Swords, and Everything Else. First, draw a card from the Everything Else pile to represent where your resistance is rooted; then, draw a Sword and work with that card's energy (referring back to this book if needed) to help you shift your mindset and cut through the source of the block.

Exercise 2

Lay out all the Sword cards on the table in front of you and choose the one that makes you most uncomfortable. Make a piece of art that expresses the discomfort you feel contemplating the card.

Exercise 3

Choose a member of the Sword court (Page, Knight, King, Queen) and a member of the Cups court. Imagine these two cards having a conversation. What can they learn from each other?

Exercise 4

Make a Swords-inspired playlist to help you energize yourself when you're dealing with difficult moments in your creative life. Choose a song for each card in the suit—ideally something that will pump you up as you work through the challenge each card offers.

The Wands

Introduction to the Wands

The Wands, otherwise known as Torches, Staffs, or Staves, are undoubtedly the tarot suit that knows how to have the most *fun*. These cards celebrate light, passion, movement, magic. This is a suit rife with enthusiasm, littered with celebrations, and full of big, unapologetic energy. The Wands' larger-than-life quality will be a welcome addition to your creative tarot tool kit.

In traditional tarot readings, Wands are often the suit most associated with creativity. While I'm arguing in this book that every single tarot card in the deck is a valuable creative conduit, there's no denying that the Wands have a special role to play when it comes to using tarot for creative pursuits.

These are the cards that will help you kick-start your imagination, generate ideas, discover new inspirations and passions, and make the most of the ones that are already filling you to the brim.

Pamela Colman Smith, the illustrator of the Rider Waite Smith deck, opted to illustrate the Wands as leaf-sprouting branches, but despite this earthy detail, the suit is ruled by the element of fire. So, consider these branches kindling to your creative flame, capable of burning bright and fervently—all you have to do is light them up.

Ultimately, the Wands can illuminate your creative path and empower you to take control of the mystical, elusive nature of creativity by recognizing it as a power in your hands, not a force that controls you.

Find Your Creative

Spark

with the *Ace of Wands*

It only takes a single match to light a fire. And it only takes one split second of inspiration to set you off on a compelling creative journey.

The Ace of Wands celebrates creative kindling, that moment of takeoff that can change everything by putting your imagination on a completely unexpected path. We've all had ideas take hold of us from seemingly nowhere at all. But that doesn't mean you should just wait around for a spark to appear.

Matches need a human hand and the rough tension of a surface to create the friction that sparks a flame. They need effort and intention. The same goes for creativity.

This Ace can help you actively spark your imagination and find compelling motivation to create, even when your creative fire isn't lighting itself.

Recognize Your Inspiration Patterns

Let the Ace of Wands be a beacon for you to follow, an opportunity to illuminate the secrets of what lights you up.

Finding the key to sparking your imagination and taking back control of your creative fire starts by recognizing patterns. If you feel an urge to create, but you don't have the ideas or the motivation to get rolling, make a list of moments in your past when you've experienced a creative spark. Where were you? What were you doing? Who were you with? What could you hear, see, taste, feel? What had you read, watched, listened to, or tried just before inspiration struck?

Exploring your past experiences may be enough to put you on a creative roll. Beyond that, reflecting on past moments of seemingly random inspiration can give you some vital information about how to engineer creative sparks in the future.

Once you get familiar with the elements that your "spark" experiences have in common, you can start to actively seek out those elements and put yourself in inspiration's way. For example, I know I have a pattern of experiencing creative breakthroughs while walking my dog without wearing headphones (or at most listening to instrumental music). It's happened enough times that now I facilitate that experience for myself intentionally.

When the Ace of Wands appears for you, reflect on what experiences have facilitated inspiration for you in the past, and how you can actively seek out that energy now.

Creative Prompts for the Ace of Wands

Make that list of past "spark" experiences and keep it available to you—as a note on your phone or a page in your notebook. Refer to it whenever you start to feel creatively dry, and see what you can do to create a new spark.

Strike a match and let the flame inspire a work of art. Freeze the fire in a photograph, or singe the edges of your collage material; create a multi-media piece that captures the flicker and crackle of the flame, or let this small light be the beginning of something more abstract.

There's an old saying about "holding a torch" for someone . . . which means holding out hope that an unrequited love will one day return your affection. Write a story about a character whose object of desire finally returns their affection, with unexpected results.

Journal about what inspiration feels like . . . in the body, the mind, the heart. Reflect on moments when you've felt inspired and look for patterns. What contributes to your moments of creative spark?

The Ace of Wands Spread

This spread is a tool for sparking your creativity. Each prompt is an opportunity to reflect on whatever ideas the card brings up for you, and how you can create from them.

Light a candle (if you can!) before shuffling your deck. Draw four cards and lay them out in the spread that follows. Then, use each card to spark your creativity—doodle, journal, or dance out your reflections on each card.

··✳ 1 ✳··

What does this card remind me of?

··✳ 2 ✳··

How does this card make me feel?

··✳ 3 ✳··

What story does this card tell me?

··✳ 4 ✳··

What detail in this card stands out to me?

Use Your Imagination

with the

Two of Wands

One seminal piece of wisdom almost every creator in the world has heard at least once is "create from what you know."

It's not *bad* advice: Looking for inspiration in what's familiar to you can help bring authenticity to your creative work. Using your own real-world experiences and observations as a foundation for your creative expression helps people connect with you and helps you ground your work in something specific and real.

Still, you shouldn't feel creatively trapped by the confines of your lived experience. You don't have to have physically seen proof of something to know it exists, and in a creative context, it's important to trust that your imagination knows what it's doing. The worlds you create in your head are, in their own way, just as real as the planet you physically inhabit. You should feel empowered to create from both the world you live in and the endless possibilities you imagine.

Enter the Two of Wands: a card that understands there's more to knowing than meets the eye. This card can empower you to straddle your real and imagined worlds, and ultimately to create meaningfully from both.

Explore More Than Your Immediate Experience

In this card, a figure stands on a castle battlement, gazing out at a landscape. They hold a wand in their left hand; another is secured to the wall behind them. Clutched in their right hand is a globe—the whole world in miniature.

This card is about understanding where you are, or creating from what you know, while simultaneously allowing yourself to see, and play, beyond your immediate surroundings. That's where imagination comes in—while the central figure of the card is located in one specific time and place of which we see a sliver, their contemplation of the globe in their hand indicates an understanding of things beyond their own specific context. They can imagine more than what they see, and they can use that knowledge to make choices and take action. In a creative context, this means feeling empowered to use both what's around you and to lean into your flights of fancy; to express what you know, but also to share what you think, which can encompass so much more than the facts of your birth and environment.

Your imagination offers you a view into a world bigger than your own—and the Two of Wands encourages you to follow that vision far and wide, to explore more than your immediate experience, to get fanciful, weird, and, of course, creative.

Creative Prompts for the Two of Wands

Find a photograph or painting you love and imagine what's going on beyond the frame. Create your own piece of visual art, or write a story, the gives a full, richly imagined picture of the wider world surrounding the original image.

Imagine a version of your life that looks very different than the life you lead day-to-day. Start by changing one detail about yourself, your circumstances, or your environment, and see how much changes as a result of that one shift. Use this imagined life to inspire a story or visual art.

Set a short story or film in a fantasy world. How can you use the power of your imagination to create a place that feels just as real as the one you live in now?

Journal about a place you'd love to go but have never been. How deep and detailed can you make your imagined trip there, even though you've never visited?

The Two of Wands Spread

This spread can help you tap into what you know and see what you can imagine. Use it whenever you want to expand the scope of a creative project.

Shuffle your deck and flip through until you find the Two of Wands. Take out the card directly in front of it and directly behind it, and lay them out in the spread that follows. Then reflect on how the cards you draw relate to the prompts in the spread.

··✳ 2 ✳··

What can I imagine?

··✳ 1 ✳··

What do I know?

See the Big Picture

III

with the Three of Wands

Sometimes, a moment of inspiration can send you down an unexpected path. While these side roads can be delightful and scenic detours, there's more to your creative journey—and more to connecting deeply to your creative passion—than dropping everything to follow any spark that glitters on the path.

To sustain a rich, creatively satisfying practice, it's important to understand how the threads you choose to follow weave together into a larger creative vision. The Three of Wands is just the card to help you see the big picture without losing sight of the delicious details that make the tapestry of your creativity unique.

In the card, a figure stands gazing out at the shoreline. Surrounding them are three wands planted firmly in the ground. In many ways, it's similar to the card that came before—the Two of Wands also features a figure surveying a vast landscape. The main difference is that in this card you're looking out in the same direction as the main character; you're sharing in their vision. You're looking out at the same sea they are, from the same vantage point, and imagining what journeys you'll take across the water. You're contemplating the world you want to build for yourself and what course you need to chart to get there.

Chart Your Course

When the Three of Wands comes up for you, use your creative thinking skills to figure out where you want to go. What sort of creative future do you want to build for yourself?

Take this card as a call to adventure, an invitation to identify and take steps toward your big-picture creative vision. You vision might be focused on turning your creative passion into a viable career or supporting other creatives as a mentor and teacher. Alternatively, your vision for a creatively satisfying life might be a deeply private and personal creative practice that is meant for no one but yourself.

There's no right or wrong. The only criteria for a creative vision is that it's something you want for yourself in the long run, and you're willing to actively take steps toward achieving it. The big picture doesn't have to mean big money or big success; it just needs to mean something important to you, something you're intentionally choosing to pursue, something that's steadily lighting your path as you push forward.

Creative Prompts for the Three of Wands

Write a letter to yourself to be opened in a year's time. Tell yourself about your creative hopes and dreams, then reflect on what writing this letter tells you now about the steps you want to take before you open this letter to read it next year.

Write a story or short film about a character with big dreams. How does their creative vision define their life choices?

Create a vision board that brings together all the elements your creative passions have in common. What themes do you notice? Use the exercise to help you clarify your creative vision and align yourself with your big-picture passions.

Journal about a creative whom you admire and what you can learn from their pursuit of their own creative vision.

The Three of Wands Spread

Use this spread to set your creative intentions when you start a new project or want to make a change in your creative life.

Flip through the Major Arcana and choose the card you feel most exemplifies what creative vision means to you. Lay that card down in response to the first spread prompt. Then, shuffle your deck and draw two more cards to complete the spread. Reflect on how the cards you draw relate to the prompts in the spread.

··✷ 1 ✷··
What is my creative vision?

··✷ 2 ✷··
How can this vision support my long-term creative satisfaction?

··✷ 3 ✷··
What can I do to help myself achieve this vision?

Know Where You Belong

with the

Four of Wands

The Four of Wands is about creating and celebrating what home feels like for you.

In the card, the four wands have been rooted in the ground, making up a canopy decorated with flowers and ribbons. Standing on the other side of the canopy, illuminated by the golden sky, two figures hold bouquets in the air, while other partygoers mill around behind them.

The bouquets and canopy are the foundation for this card's historic association with marriage. Over time, that interpretation has been abstracted to represent any meaningful celebration that brings people together. But this card is about so much more than one party on one day; it's about the sense of belonging that the party celebrates and fosters. In a creative context, this can be a card about recognizing, celebrating, and building on the belonging you experience when you truly connect to your creativity. You and your creativity belong together. You always have; you always will.

Your Creativity Will Always Be Here

Let's break down the key elements in this card:

First, there's the canopy. In many cultures a wedding canopy is a metaphor for the home and life that the newlyweds will build together. It represents stability, comfort, and, because we are dealing with the Wands, passion—all foundations for a lasting relationship. When you transfer this metaphor to your creative life, the canopy can stand in for the way you build a creative practice that feels like home for you.

Then, there's the two waving figures: Depending on how you read the card, you might see them waving you off on an adventure or welcoming you home. Either way, the same promise is inherent in their gesture: You belong here, and whether you are coming or going, you will always be warmly welcomed. The same goes for your creativity: Whether you're taking a step away from your creative pursuits, coming back to your creative practice after a break, or showing up for the very first time, you are always welcome.

Finally, there's the partygoers in the background. These figures don't take up much space; you might miss them if you don't look closely, and that's important. Their presence as supporters is secondary to your relationship with your creativity. These are your guests— the people you invite into your creative world. But they are peripheral in comparison to the private creative experience that sustains you.

Whenever you draw this card, take a moment to come home to your personal passions and creative desires, and trust that your creativity will always be there for you.

Creative Prompts for the Four of Wands

Throw a party that celebrates your creative practice. But don't wait for a massive milestone to do it. Throw it this week or this month, just because.

Design your own canopy to represent the sense of belonging you've built for yourself through your creative practice. Make it in 3D, or sketch it out, or use collage, but make it your own.

Use weddings as a theme to inspire a piece of art. Set a story or film at a wedding, paint the nuptials of your dreams, or arrange a flower bouquet you can use to decorate your home.

Journal about what it means to feel at home in your creative practice. In what ways does your creative experience already feel like home? How might you deepen that sense of belonging?

The Four of Wands Spread

Your creativity always belongs to you, and vice versa. Use this spread to help you explore the ways you and your creativity are intimately connected.

Shuffle your deck and split it into two stacks. Take a card off the top of each stack and lay them out in the spread that follows. Then reflect on how the cards you draw relate to the prompts in the spread.

· ✳ 1 ✳ ·

How do I belong to my creativity?

· ✳ 2 ✳ ·

How does my creativity belong to me?

Brainstorm Effectively

with the

V

Five of Wands

The Five of Wands is one of the most dynamic cards in the deck. In the image, five figures spar with their wands, and the resulting action appears chaotic and contradictory.

At first glance, it might look like battle, but on close inspection you'll see that the scene is more like a scrimmage or an energetic game.

While traditionally this card is said to symbolize conflict among groups, it's not a particularly threatening image. There's no hint of actual violence, nothing close to the ominous battle scenes common throughout the suit of Swords. The figures in the card seem to be taking the whole business in a playful stride. It gives the impression of a classroom where everyone is raising their hands at once—loud, chaotic, excited, brimming with possibility.

All of that considered, I like to think of this card's imagery as the physical manifestation of a brainstorm.

Entertain ALL the Ideas

If the Wands represent your passions, your ideas, your creative spark, then this card illustrates what it's like to have many different creative possibilities stirring around and vying for your attention.

An effective brainstorming session is all about giving yourself the opportunity to envision any and every possibility, to give every idea a chance. So, when you draw the Five of Wands, it's an invitation to make time to engage with and generate creative ideas—big, small, "good," "bad," and everything in between. This card celebrates, without judgment or discrimination, all the amazing creative things your mind can cook up when you give it the space and time.

Brainstorming is one of the most fundamental tools in any creative's arsenal. Whether you need to figure out what happens next in your screenplay, come up with outfits to wear to an event, devise a solution to a client brief, draft a menu for a dinner party, or solve an unexpected problem at work, the first step is to lay out all the ideas on the table. And I do mean ALL the ideas.

Entertaining all the options, whether you eventually judge them good enough or not, is an important step in the creative process. It helps you recognize all of the different possibilities, notice patterns, and combine ideas until you've got the right solution. And when you think of the Five of Wands as a manifestation of that excited, anything-goes vibe, then you can dive into problem-solving with high energy and an open mind.

Creative Prompts for the Five of Wands

For any current project where you feel stuck, make a list of the twenty most ridiculous directions you could take. Choose one ridiculous direction and follow through, just to see what happens.

Come up with the worst creative idea you've ever had. Turn it into a game; how far can you push your bad idea? How can you make having bad ideas fun?

Create your own version of this card, but first . . . brainstorm five different concepts for how you can recreate the card in your own way. Then choose one.

Journal about what tools help you brainstorm effectively and how you can make those tools more readily available for yourself anytime you feel creatively stuck.

The Five of Wands Spread

This spread offers a fun and simple way to practice brainstorming and idea generation, and you can make use of it anytime, whether you're feeling stuck or just want to have a little low-pressure creative fun.

You'll need a timer, your tarot deck, and somewhere to take notes. Shuffle your deck and draw one card, placing it face down on the table in front of you. Set the timer for two minutes, then jot down all of the ideas you have in response to the prompt until the timer goes off. Do the same for the following cards.

1

Four stories this card inspires me to tell

2

Three pieces of visual art this card inspires me to make

3

Two adventures this card inspires me to go on

4

One gift this card inspires me to give

Create Like You've

VI

Already Won

with
the

Six of
Wands

Despite its reputation as a harbinger of bad omens, the tarot loves a good win. A number of cards throughout the deck deal in victory and triumph—the Queen of Swords, the Three and Nine of Cups, the World, and the Six of Wands. In fact, when the twentieth-century occultists Aleister Crowley and Lady Frieda Harris developed their popular Thoth tarot deck, they inscribed the word "victory" directly onto this card.

The Six of Wands looks like the platonic ideal of "winning"—it's a literal victory parade. The central figure, our hero, rides across the card on a white horse. They sport a laurel crown on their head, and a victory wreath is hung from the tip of their wand. Behind and around them, their supporters cheer, raising their own wands into the air.

It's a fantasy of how any creative hopes to feel when you complete a project or put your work out into the world: like you've won.

Every Creative Impulse Is a Jackpot

Generally speaking, I don't advise judging your creativity on a win/lose rubric. The creative experience exists outside that binary. There's no real winning or losing in creativity; there's only exploring, experiencing, and evolving.

But maybe there is one way to win in a creative context: by recognizing your natural inclination toward creativity for the jackpot it is. Your impulse to create is a miracle; it's magic; it's everything. What if winning at creativity isn't about points earned, profits made, the best idea, or the best execution? What if winning were all about living a joyfully creative life?

Every creative impulse is a lottery win and every choice you make to honor those impulses is a victory. Create like you've already won the game, because you're here, you're creating. You are breathing life into the magic inside your head, and isn't that the biggest win any of us could hope for?

Coming into creative ventures and projects as if you're already on top—simply because you're enjoying the opportunity to engage with your creativity—will change the way you create forever. If you're willing to see that you're already the victor, you'll waste so much less time doubting yourself, so much less energy watering down your vision or overcompensating because you're afraid that what you have to offer isn't enough.

The Six of Wands says create like a winner, because if you're creating at all, you are one.

Creative Prompts for the Six of Wands

Design yourself a trophy that celebrates you as a winner simply for being creative.

Choregraph a victory dance inspired by the sports heroes who celebrate their wins through physical expression (if you haven't seen Chicago Bulls player Chuck Swirsky's iconic victory dance, google it, and start from there).

Write a poem or song as an ode to your creative victories.

Journal about your current creative endeavor as if you've already accomplished what you've set out to do. Pay attention to how this builds your confidence.

The Six of Wands Spread

Turn to this spread anytime you need a pep talk or a reminder of the many ways you're already doing things right in your creative life.

Shuffle your deck, hold it against your heart, and tell yourself—out loud—that you're doing an amazing job. Then draw three cards and lay them out in the spread that follows. Reflect on how the cards you draw relate to the prompts in the spread.

··✳ 1 ✳··

How am I already winning in my creative life?

··✳ 2 ✳··

How can I celebrate what I'm doing right in my creative life?

··✳ 3 ✳··

How can I keep building my creative confidence?

Defend Yourself from
Distraction

VII

with
the

Seven
of
Wands

The Seven of Wands often comes up when you're struggling to finish a project, not because you're blocked, but because other shiny new ideas, opportunities, or tasks are jostling for your attention. Sometimes a shiny new thing looks like a fully fledged new project idea; sometimes it looks like a rabbit-hole research deep dive that you're sure will be useful somehow, someday; sometimes it looks like a run-of-the-mill distraction—a crisis at work that isn't actually as urgent as you're telling yourself it is, or a task that could wait for later (who among us hasn't spent time planning a vacation when we're supposed to be focusing on an upcoming deadline?).

This experience is completely normal. If I had a dollar for every client who came in for a reading about one creative project and ended up telling me about six other ideas or "urgent" things instead, I could have retired from my tarot business by now. I always ask them the same thing: "This feeling of urgency you're experiencing around new pursuits . . . is it about really needing to move on from what you're working on, or are you courting distraction because you're afraid of following through on something?"

Sometimes their answer is the former, but a lot of times it's the latter. If you fall into the latter camp, then the Seven of Wands can help you recognize what's going on for you and what you want to do about it.

Stick It Out

To do the hard work of staying on course, the Seven of Wands encourages you to keep your current project close. The figure in the card is using their wand to fend off all the others that are vying for their attention, and you can do the same—keep your current project in your hands, and when you're tempted to start something new, use the impulse to recommit to your current project instead.

Keep something that represents your primary goal as close to you as possible. If it's something you can keep in a notebook, carry the notebook around with you. If that doesn't work, pick a talisman like a piece of jewelry or a temporary tattoo you can wear on your person to remind you that you're committed to completing your current project.

When you draw this card, take it as a personal endorsement from the tarot for what you're working on—the cards want to see it finished; they believe in your ability to stick it out.

Creative Prompts for the Seven of Wands

Spend ten minutes, right now, making progress on a current project. Just open the document, add a brushstroke, send a text to a collaborator, or order new supplies. Whatever small step you can take now to recommit to the thing you're working toward, do it.

Write yourself an email listing all of the things distracting you from your most important creative pursuit. Schedule the email to be sent to you in a week or month's time, and deal with it then.

Call a friend and ask them to give you a pep talk about why you need to stick this project out. If you're creating in secret, be your own friend—write yourself a letter detailing why this project deserves to be finished.

Journal in response to this question: Is the feeling of urgency I'm experiencing around new pursuits really about needing to move on from what I'm working on, or am I courting distraction because I'm afraid of following through on something?

The Seven of Wands Spread

Whenever you need to defend against distractions and recommit to your creative priority, this spread has your back.

Shuffle your deck and flip through until you find the Seven of Wands. Then draw the three cards behind it and lay them out in the spread that follows. Then reflect on how the cards you draw relate to the prompts in the spread.

· ✳ 1 ✳ ·

How can I recommit to the project I need to finish?

· ✳ 2 ✳ ·

How can I put aside my distractions for the time being?

· ✳ 3 ✳ ·

Where can I seek out support to help me stay the course?

Start and Finish Strong

with the

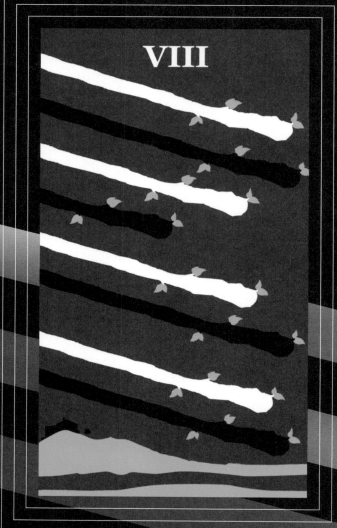

VIII

Eight of Wands

The painter Jean-Michel Basquiat famously summed up his process in a simple sentence: "I start a picture and I finish it."

Of course, there's so much that happens in the middle to stitch that start and finish together, but Basquiat's Cliff Notes on the life cycle of a creative project hits on something important: the critical role of the start and the finish.

Depending on how you look at it (and in what context you draw it), the Eight of Wands can symbolize either the impassioned beginning or the frenzied end of a creative project. (To help you figure out whether your focus should be endings or beginnings, whenever you draw the card, ask yourself: Do I see the wands sailing toward the ground or taking off into the air?)

Beginnings and endings take a special kind of energy and alignment. Notice how all eight wands move through the air in harmony with each other. There's a synergy here, a sense of connection that helps kick things off on the right foot, and then brings things neatly to the ground when the end is in sight.

Start as You Mean to Go On

When this card comes up in the context of a beginning, it's an opportunity for you to reflect on whatever creative journey you're getting ready to depart on. That might be a new piece of art, a course, a partnership, a business launch. Now is the time to get your ducks in a row so you can start strong. Get clear on what you want to achieve through this new endeavor so that you feel confident in how you're approaching it. Consider, too, what it will take for the other areas of your life to align with the creative goals you're setting. Will you need support from anyone in your life while you step into this new beginning?

When the card comes up in the context of finishing a project, or wrapping up a part of your creative life so you can move on to something new, give yourself time to reflect on what a satisfying ending would feel like for you. Are there still questions you want to answer for yourself, elements of the project you want to refine, or connections you want to solidify before you move on? Make sure you've got all your loose ends as tied up as possible and focus on prioritizing the actions that will help you make it to the end of this chapter of your creative life in a way that makes you proud.

And, most importantly, whether you're starting or finishing, stay closely attuned to the passions that are driving your creative actions. Let that sense of vitality and vision be the fuel that keeps you aloft and the compass that brings you back home.

Creative Prompts for the Eight of Wands

Think about the beginning of your favorite song, story, or film. What makes it so special? Take what you learn about strong beginnings by reflecting on your favorite examples and create your own strong start to a project.

Script a short film or play that begins in reverse. Start at the end and move backward in time, until the story comes to a close at the beginning.

Make two playlists—one for beginnings and one for endings. Play them to pump yourself up when you're starting or finishing a project.

Journal about the most meaningful beginnings and endings in your own life.

The Eight of Wands Spread

Use this spread to reflect on the beginnings and endings you're stepping into now.

Divide your deck into four stacks and shuffle each separately. Then, draw a card from each stack and lay all four out in the spread that follows. Reflect on how the cards you draw relate to the prompts in the spread.

··✳ 1 ✳··
What beginnings are taking place in my creative life right now?

··✳ 2 ✳··
How can I get things started off right?

··✳ 3 ✳··
What's coming to an end in my creative life right now?

··✳ 4 ✳··
How can I finish strong?

Navigate Creative Competition and Envy

with the

IX

Nine of Wands

The Nine of Wands can feel a little ominous. The claustrophobic image of a wounded figure is uncomfortable, and it may remind you of moments on your creative journey where you've felt unsupported, actively sabotaged, or victimized by others.

But in classic tarot fashion, the discomfort this card stirs up is actually designed to help you dig into something meaningful. Be brave enough to sit with what this card brings up, and you'll come out the other side of the Nine of Wands wiser, more self-aware, and more creatively empowered than when you first flipped the card over.

Give yourself space to explore what this card has to say to you about competition and envy. Take in the way the wounded central figure eyes the wands behind them, as if they are the enemy, creeping up to destroy them. In response, the central figure clings even harder to their own wand. When you think about it in the context of envy and competition, the card becomes less an indication of incoming attack and more an illustration of clinging to a fear of being overtaken.

Harness Your Jealousy

Navigating competition and jealousy in your creative life is normal, especially if you're putting yourself out there and sharing your work. You might envy the praise and opportunities you see others receiving, or you may covet another creative's talent or the privileges that have allowed them to prioritize their creativity over other pursuits.

If you're experiencing creative jealousy or finding yourself caught up in competition, you're not a bad person—you're actually in very good company. Take the essayist Roxane Gay, who has written often about her creative "nemeses." If a *New York Times* best-selling author can hold space for herself to experience jealousy, then you're allowed to, too.

The trick is to harness that jealousy into something productive, instead of letting it eat at you. Gay turns her jealousy into creative expression; she uses her experiences of envy and competition to fuel her writing, to get playful with her feelings, and to relate to her readers. The Nine of Wands is offering you the opportunity to do the same. You can accept that your jealousy and creative competitiveness exist; you can own them and even find inspiration in them. You can refuse to let them put out your creative spark.

When this card appears, you're invited to survey your jealousies and reframe them as fuel for your own creative fire. Instead of letting yourself fall prey to all the ways you think you're missing out or getting buried under other people's success, you can remember yourself and refuse to let other creatives' wins distract you from your own creative satisfaction.

Creative Prompts for the Nine of Wands

Jealousy has been referred to as the "green-eyed monster." Create your own version of the monster in a piece of art. You can draw it, paint it, draft an epic poem about it, script a short film, or even turn yourself into the monster through makeup design.

Create a self-portrait depicting you as the source of someone else's jealousy. Pay attention to how this exercise forces you to pay attention to your strengths and wins.

Make a list of qualities your creative peers possess that you are jealous of. What can these qualities teach you about what you really want from your creative life?

Journal about your biggest creative "nemesis"—who is it, and why do they get under your skin? How can you reframe your rivalry into creative inspiration?

The Nine of Wands Spread

This spread can help you explore healthy ways of managing and reframing your jealousies.

Shuffle your deck and draw three cards. Lay the cards out in the spread that follows, then reflect on how the cards you draw relate to the prompts in the spread.

··✳ 1 ✳··
How is creative envy holding me back right now?

··✳ 2 ✳··
What can I learn from the envy I'm experiencing?

··✳ 3 ✳··
What quality do my creative peers envy in me?

Don't Lose Sight of Your Vision

X

with the Ten of Wands

If you've ever packed sixteen outfits for a three-day trip in a bid to make sure you've got all your favorite options available to you (just in case!), then the Ten of Wands' vibe probably feels familiar. This card is about coming in way too hot on way too much, and cramming your creative suitcase so full of potential looks that it gets too heavy to carry.

In the card, a character struggles with a bushel of ten wands. At some point, collecting all those wands probably seemed like a good idea. But somewhere along the way, they've taken on so much that their back has started to bow beneath the weight, and they've completely obscured their view of the road in front of them. They've overdone it, and they're at risk of tripping themselves up and losing it all.

Creative people tend to treat ideas and opportunities this way, hoarding everything that comes along our path, leaving every mental tab open, just in case. Many of us are "yes" people—we want to try things, we want to see where an opportunity will take us. But we're not always good at recognizing that even though saying yes can open up all kinds of exciting new potential, *too much* yes can also close us off to what we really want for our creative life.

Reconnect to Your Priorities

When this card appears, it would be easy to take it as a rebuke. It feels like the tarot wagging its finger at you, saying, "You messed up and bit off more than you can chew." But in reality, this card wants to be your ally. When you draw it, think of it as the tarot's way of asking if you're OK, because the burden you're carrying looks awfully heavy.

What the Ten of Wands is really asking you to do is recognize when you've taken on too much and question whether you really need to be carrying it all right now. It's a reminder to prioritize.

Whenever you see it, take a moment to check in with your big-picture creative vision (see the Three of Wands); ask yourself which ideas and opportunities will best serve you in pursuing that vision and which ones you can put aside so you can see the path ahead more clearly.

Creative Prompts for the Ten of Wands

Make an "ideas for later" box.
Every time you find yourself racking up new ideas and opportunities, write them down on a slip of paper and store them in your ideas box, so you can come back to them when you've got the mental space.

Make a poster or piece of art
that represents your big-picture creative vision and put it somewhere you can see it. Whenever you start to feel too overloaded, refer to this illustration of your vision and ask yourself: Which of my creative pursuits are serving this vision and which are preventing me from getting here?

Take a day off from everything.
Set all your wands down and give your mind, body, and creativity the rest they deserve. Give yourself the gift of fully clearing your mind and taking the pressure off yourself to carry anything at all, even the important stuff.

Journal about what your top ten creative priorities are. Then whittle the list down from ten to five.

The Ten of Wands Spread

If you're feeling overburdened and unsure of how to readjust your load so that you can move ahead without breaking your back, drop everything and pull out this spread.

Shuffle your deck ten times, then draw three cards. Reflect on how the cards you draw relate to the prompts in the spread.

·✳ 1 ✳·	·✳ 2 ✳·	·✳ 3 ✳·
What creative priority can I set aside right now?	What creative priority do I want to keep pursuing?	How can this prioritization support my bigger creative picture?

Reclaim Your Attention

with the

Page of Wands

The Page of Wands is a mascot for the art of attention.

You can tell by the way the figure in this image investigates the wand in their hand that they could be just as fascinated by a brick, a clod of dirt, a discoloration on the wall. Their indiscriminate curiosity knows no bounds, and they satisfy that curiosity through attention.

That combination of wide-ranging curiosity and abundant attention is a creative's best friend (my neurodivergent pals might also recognize these as the key ingredients for hyperfocus). Attention breeds ideation and craft—the more of it you give to the moment you're in, the more depth, knowledge, experience, and imagination you can bring to your creative expression.

Be Present in Your Process

From billboard ads to phone games to incessant work communications to the daily admin of being a human, the gift of attention is more precious than we give it credit for. It takes dedication and practice to reclaim your attention and curiosity, but it is possible to learn how to be creative with your attention, even when it feels like the world is against you.

One way to reclaim your attention is to practice being present and mindful during the act of creating. True creativity requires presence—for you to be fully *there* with your ideas and your tools. And presence is all about giving your attention to the moment, to the vibration of a finger plucking a guitar string, the sound of a paintbrush's bristles stroking the canvas.

Reading tarot is another excellent way to practice attention. Try sitting with a card for as long as you can, scoping out all of the tiniest details. What can you notice in two minutes? Five minutes? Ten?

When the Page of Wands appears in a reading, it reminds you that the more attention you can afford to your life, the more you'll be rewarded in your creative pursuits. A lifetime of attention helps you make unique connections, see creative opportunities where others can't, and evolve your process as you continue to observe your world with voracious curiosity.

Creative Prompts for the Page of Wands

Pick up the closest item to you and see how long you can spend describing it in detail. Every time you think there's nothing else to describe, challenge yourself to write one more line.

Take ten minutes to do a mindfulness meditation. You can find plenty online, but the simplest thing to do it close your eyes and mentally scan through your body bit by bit. Try to afford attention to every piece of yourself individually, down to each eyelash and finger-nail. Afterward, write about or sketch out what it feels like to give your body your undivided attention.

Pick a topic and spend an afternoon learning everything you can about it. Your topic can be anything that interests you, but keep it narrow. Mine might be medieval Italian playing card decks. Yours might be the history of a certain food, the entire discography of a band you just discovered, a rare species of fish, or a very specific skill you've always wanted to learn. Whatever you choose, give it your full, undivided attention.

Journal about your relationship with attention. What are your typical distractions? What in your life takes up the bulk of your attention, and are you happy with that? What do you wish you had infinite attention for?

The Page of Wands Spread

This one-card spread is designed to help you practice the art of pay-ing attention in a generative, creative way. Use it anytime you need to reset and reposition yourself in the now.

Shuffle your cards. Do it slowly, really taking notice of the way the cards feel in your hands. When you're ready, draw a card and lay it out on the table. Give it your full attention and notice everything you possibly can about the image before interpreting the message the card has to offer. Pay attention, too, to how the things you notice about the card and the way you interpret it make you feel. Then, reflect on what you see in the card and what it's telling you.

> ·✳ 1 ✳·
>
> What is this card inviting me to pay more attention to in my creative life?

Have a Creative Fling

with the **Knight of Wands**

The Knight of Wands is considered the "playboy" of the tarot. For many readers, it represents short-lived but highly passionate relationships—flings of epic proportions. It's not so different in a creative context, with the added bonus that a *creative* fling is much less likely to break your heart.

Having a "creative fling" looks like stepping back from whatever creative endeavor you're currently enmeshed in and taking some time to pursue something else *just for fun*. If you've recently found yourself on creative autopilot, it's prime time for the Knight of Wands to come swanning in and take you on the adventure of your life.

This card presents an exercise in letting your creativity have whatever it wants, instead of assigning it tasks to complete. If you want to fingerpaint, the Knight of Wands says go for it. If you've never written a book but have been itching to try, the Knight of Wands will jump into the deep end with you. If you want to rekindle a love for baking rather than strategizing about expanding your creative business, the Knight of Wands loves that for you (and happily volunteers to taste test).

Give Yourself Over to Creative Desire

Keep in mind that a creative fling doesn't have to mean switching gears to *make* something new. It can also be about giving yourself permission to step back and let your creativity *consume* what it wants. Maybe your creativity wants to go somewhere you've never been and soak up the vibes; maybe it wants to lie down in the grass and listen to the entire discography of your favorite artist; maybe it wants to go swimming or try every almond croissant in town until it has identified the best one (a real creative fling I once found myself in the throes of).

The important takeaway from the Knight of Wands is that it's not "bad" or "irresponsible" to let yourself get carried away for a bit. You're allowed—nay, encouraged—to get swept up in a moment of surprise passion. These are the gifts that keep your creativity alive, that feed and nurture the hungry, adventurous part of you at the very root of your creative experience.

The Knight of Wands won't stick around forever; sooner or later they'll leave you for new pastures, but they won't leave you with nothing. They'll leave you with the fresh memory of what it feels like to give yourself over to pure creative pleasure. And that gift is something you can bring back to your daily practice and your long-term creative ambitions.

Creative Prompts for the Knight of Wands

Sign up for a creative workshop. You can find plenty of options online and in person within your community. Make sure that whatever you're signing up for is something new and exciting for you.

Take yourself on a solo adventure. Depending on your resources, you might book a full-on trip or just plan a visit to a local place you've never been to. Let yourself be swept up in the newness of the experience.

Recreate your own version of this card in a creative medium you don't normally work in. Do it for fun, and nothing else.

Journal about what it feels like to get carried away with your creativity, to give yourself the freedom and permission to get swept up and lost in something new.

The Knight of Wands Spread

In a creative rut? Turn to this spread to reignite your flame and bring a little bit of adventure into your creative life.

Shuffle your deck and then flip through until you find the Knight of Wands. Take the first card behind the Knight and place it down in the first position of the spread. Then, shuffle again and flip through until you find the Knight again, placing the card behind the Knight down in the second spread position. Repeat the process for the third spread position. Then, reflect on how the cards you draw relate to the prompts in the spread.

·❋ 1 ❋·

What element of my creative life is on autopilot?

·❋ 2 ❋·

How can I escape my creative routine right now?

·❋ 3 ❋·

How will a moment of escape revitalize my creative practice?

Keep Your Spark Alive

with the

King of Wands

Kings in the tarot are paragons of success. They've mastered the energy of their suit and wield it as a tool to their advantage. The King of Wands is no different; here we see a King who has strategically followed their passions all the way to the top. They have tuned into their creative vision, generated ideas to help them achieve that vision, and stayed the course with passionate dedication.

If you're drawing this card, congratulations. You've done really well for yourself. You've stuck to your creative vision and now you're reaping the benefits.

But, achieving creative success can be a double-edged sword (or maybe more appropriately here, a double-ended wand). Fulfilling a creative vision can leave you questioning your identity and wondering, *what now*? For some creatives, the more successful you become in your creative career, the less connected you find yourself to the creative process that first lit you up. You might be at a loss for how to keep your creative spark alive in this new era of your creative journey.

That's where the King of Wands can teach you a thing or two.

Stay in the Game

This King is not a passive monarch. They're a warrior; they lead from experience. They came into their position because they've been genuinely engaged and active on their climb through the ranks. Being King may never have been this figure's vision, but being the best version of themselves always has been, and so they've found themself here, at the top of their game. And they know that the best way to stay on top is to stay *in* the game . . . to resist becoming a spectator or a judge, to keep on playing for the love of it.

Everything about this card indicates the King's dedication to staying engaged with their own creative process, to never forget what it's like to be striving and burning for something they want. Look at the way they sit at the edge of their seat, ready to leap back into battle at any point. And look how their torch is planted on the ground, not on the elevated platform where they sit, indicating a deep-rooted connection to where they came from. This King's power doesn't come from their position. It comes from their own passion and experience.

When this card appears, it's a prompt to connect with your roots. Stay in touch with what brings you creative joy, even if you've graduated beyond it in a professional sense. Don't lose sight of those early sparks; they're some of the most powerful fuel you have to sustain a creative life for the long term.

Creative Prompts for the King of Wands

Write a story or short film about a character who is at the top of their game. What do they stand to lose now? How are they a different version of themselves from when they started out?

Share an old piece of creative work with friends, family, or your wider audience. Let them in on the story of this project, how it helped you progress as a creative, and why you still feel connected to it now.

Take yourself back to basics by reacquainting yourself with a beginner's task in a medium you know well. Musicians might return to basic chords, writers might play with simple rhymes, photographers might revert to the simplicity of a Polaroid camera. How does it feel to reconnect with the raw fundamentals of your creative pursuits?

Journal about where you started versus where you are now in your creative journey. Consider how you've grown, but also what you'd like to reconnect with from your early days.

The King of Wands Spread

If you're killing it in your creative life but want to make sure you don't lose sight of the spark that set you on your creative journey in the first place, crack this spread out.

Shuffle your deck and hold the cards against your heart for a beat before drawing three and laying them out in the spread that follows. Then reflect on how the cards you draw relate to the prompts in the spread.

1. How have I evolved and succeeded in my creative life?

3. How can I keep my creative spark alive?

2. How can I stay connected to my creative roots?

Take Up Space

with
the
Queen of
Wands

In the tarot, Queens are symbols of an internal mastery of the element that the suit represents. That means the Queen of Wands represents a sense of inner confidence when it comes to your creative passion and vision. Looking at this image, you can't deny that the creative confidence of the Queen of Wands, the surety she places in her own passion and vision, is off the charts.

The throne's leonine motif nods to the fierce regality of this character's presence; the warm colors and sunflowers represent the Queen's passionate energy; and the cat at the Queen's feet hints at magic, putting power directly into the Queen's hands.

Then there's the body language. This is the only Queen in the tarot to face front; the others we get in profile, as if they're holding something back, protecting themselves from the viewer.

The Queen of Wands, by contrast, unabashedly takes up not just the full seat of the throne but also the full frame of the image, displaying themself head-on for the viewer's attention. "Here I am," says the Queen. "Aren't I absolutely radiant?"

Own Your Creative Power

This card counsels you to show up loud, proud, and comfortable in your skin.

You might worry that taking up space equates to setting yourself up for failure, that owning your creative power or talking up your creative work is just generating expectations you feel like you can never reach. To this the Queen of Wands says: You don't need anyone's permission or approval to step into your creative power. You can give that permission and approval to yourself.

If it's not a fear of failure holding you back from accessing your inner Queen of Wands, your resistance might be rooted in a fear of appearing self-absorbed. But, never forget, you are the biggest and most influential advocate for your own work. It is your job to be proud of your creativity, to acknowledge your own glamour.

You are allowed, and very much encouraged by the Queen of Wands, to show off, to put your creative expression, identity, and vision in front of other people and say, "Here it is. Isn't it radiant?"

When you draw the Queen of Wands, let the card feel like the jackpot it is. Take the Queen's appearance as the pep talk you need to show up in the world loud, proud, and unabashedly your full creative self. Fiercely and confidently share your magic, knowing it's worthwhile— for you, and for others.

Creative Prompts for the Queen of Wands

Write an acceptance speech for a creative award you'd love to win. Channel the Queen of Wands' confidence to imagine yourself in this celebrated position one day.

Practice taking up more space with your body, like the Queen of Wands does. How does it feel to claim more space instead of making yourself feel small?

Design a crown that represents this Queen's regal confidence. Incorporate the symbols within the card—like the sunflower, the lions, and the cat—into your design. Bonus points for snapping a self-portrait of yourself wearing the crown.

Journal about a Queen of Wands figure in your life. What can you learn from them about confidence, boldness, and ferocity?

The Queen of Wands Spread

Embrace your inner Queen of Wands confidence with this spread. Turn to it anytime you need a pep talk.

Pull the Queen of Wands out of the deck and shuffle while looking at the card, taking in its confident, passionate energy. When you're ready, draw four cards and lay them out in the spread that follows. Reflect on how the cards you draw relate to the prompts in the spread.

··❋ 1 ❋··

What creative quality do I deserve to show off?

··❋ 3 ❋··

How can I motivate myself to show off and take up space?

··❋ 4 ❋··

How can Queen of Wands energy help me grow in my creative life?

··❋ 2 ❋··

What's holding me back from taking up space?

WANDS EXERCISES

Exercise 1

Look back to the Major Arcana and pick out two or three cards that feel most thematically similar to the suit of Wands. Then journal about figures in your real life, or in pop culture and history, who fit into this theme, too. What can you learn from these people about creativity, vision, and passion?

Exercise 2

The Wands go by many names in different tarot decks. Sometimes they are the Torches, the Staffs, the Batons, the Clubs . . . how does each name enrich your understanding of the Wands as tools of creative passion and vision?

Exercise 3

Spend a day acting as if you were your favorite member of the Wands court (Page, Knight, King, Queen). How can living like this character help bring your creative spark to life?

Exercise 4

The Wands are associated with fire energy. Go shopping for a candle that you're drawn to because of its smell or design. Light this candle whenever you want to infuse some passion and vision into your creative practice.

The Pentacles

Introduction to the Pentacles

As the suit representing material things and earthly matters, the Pentacles offer the perfect counterbalance to the deep emotional, spiritual, and mental work inspired by the Cups, Swords, and Wands. The Pentacles, which resemble (and in some decks are called) coins, are about planting the seeds you've gathered over the course of this book and nurturing them to life through thoughtful action. This suit will help you turn your tarot adventure into a part of your daily life, so that caring for your creativity becomes a routine without ever losing its magic.

The Pentacles are an essential tool for your creativity. These cards are a reminder that hard work, patience, care, and sustenance—the "boring," down-to-earth aspects of your creative life—can yield real transformative magic.

Without the Pentacles' practicality, creativity is trapped in daydreams. You and your creativity deserve more than that. These cards will guide you in finding ways for your creativity and your daily life to work together, instead of forever competing for your attention.

Summon the energy of the Pentacles whenever you feel bored, stalled, or stuck. They'll bring their tough, rational love to the table to remind you that you have the power to infuse life into your creative process again, through the simple magic of showing up and being present and intentional with your creativity.

Nurture **Your Creative Gifts**

with the **Ace of Pentacles**

Like all the Aces in the tarot, the Ace of Pentacles welcomes you into a new suit by offering a gift. In the traditional imagery of the card, you see a hand extending from the ether, cupped around a glowing coin. This is an offering—the gift of the sun breaking through clouds, an unexpected opportunity to shine.

As a suit, the Pentacles are associated with material things, so it's nice to think of this card, even more than all the other Aces, as a physical gift. Imagine being presented with something that takes your creativity to the next level, all wrapped up and beautiful, ready for you to enjoy.

A creative gift might come in the form of a canceled meeting that gives you an unplanned moment to pick up your sketchbook, knitting needles, or baking tools, or even just to daydream. The gift might be something truly material—a new set of paints, a ticket to an event you want to attend, a new outfit that has that special power to make you feel more creative. And, of course, the gift might be an idea, something that pops unexpectedly into your head on your commute, washes over you in the shower, or comes to you in a dream.

However the gift arrives, the Ace of Pentacles challenges you not only to recognize it for what it is, but also to protect and nourish it so it achieves its full potential.

Give Back

While the glimmering gifted pentacle dominates most of the card's imagery, the walled garden that grounds and frames the image is equally important. The garden is more than a decorative element—it's an important instruction for what to do with your creative gifts: Cultivate and care for them. Build a garden for your creativity to keep your ideas, projects, and opportunities safe, nurtured, and accessible.

After all, that brilliant shower thought is only one half of the gift. You have been offered a seed, but if you want that seed to flower, you have to give it gifts in return: You have to plant it, water it, protect it, and prune it. What good is a gift stuck in the back of the closet, untended to and gathering dust?

When you draw the Ace of Pentacles, be on the lookout for the seeds that are carried by the wind into your airspace. Keep your eyes peeled for the gift of potential, and return that present with a gift of your own: attention, care, and respect.

Creative Prompts for the Ace of Pentacles

Make a gift for someone you love, using your creative talents. Write them a song, draw them a picture, sculpt them a vase and pop their favorite flower inside, design a piece of jewelry just for them. Enjoy the experience of being generous with your creativity.

Script a short film about an exchange of gifts—cast one character who gives and receives graciously, and another who shows no gratitude or generosity. Think about how these opposing behaviors can drive conflict.

Make a wish list of gifts you'd like to give your creativity: a weekend retreat, a new set of paintbrushes, a course, a book, a bouquet of flowers—anything that would delight your inner artist. Choose the most inexpensive item on the list and purchase it.

Journal about a time when a creative idea came to you unbidden. How did you make the most of that gift? How can you revisit that gift now?

The Ace of Pentacles Spread

Use this spread to identify the creative gifts you're being offered, and reflect on ways you can nurture those gifts.

Shuffle your deck and flip through until you find the Ace of Pentacles. Draw out the two cards just behind the Ace and lay them down in the spread that follows. Then reflect on how the cards you draw relate to the prompts in the spread.

```
┌──────────────┐   ┌──────────────┐
│   ·❋ 1 ❋·     │   │   ·❋ 2 ❋·     │
│              │   │              │
│              │   │              │
│ What creative│   │  How can I   │
│ gift am I    │   │ nurture that │
│ being        │   │    gift?     │
│ offered?     │   │              │
│              │   │              │
└──────────────┘   └──────────────┘
```

Balance Your Priorities

with the

II

Two of Pentacles

If you find it difficult to prioritize your creativity when it feels like so many other things—paying bills, getting the kids to school, keeping the house clean, maintaining relationships, literally every other responsibility in your life—must be dealt with first, you're not alone.

Making creativity a priority is a struggle for many creatives—hobbyists *and* professionals.

No matter what your creative aspirations are, there will be times in your life (probably many times!) where your creative dreams feel at odds with everything else you have to do to make your life work. Creativity demands a lot of brain space, attention, and commitment. So, too, does surviving in this world.

The Two of Pentacles offers validation for that struggle. The illustration of a juggler, passing two pentacles back and forth for eternity, symbolizes the perpetual balancing act of managing your creativity and the practicalities of your life.

But the card also offers hope. Its playful disposition suggests that striking that necessary balance doesn't have to be a drag.

Find Your Own Rhythm

While navigating the balance between your creative dreams and the other demands of your life rarely feels like a day at the beach, the Two of Pentacles asks, "But what if you turned it into one?" This card is all about recognizing the inevitable balance you have to strike, accepting there will be a constant back and forth, and gamifying it.

How can you make the interplay between your creative aspirations and the responsibilities of your life fun and engaging?

Some creatives are dedicated to making their calendars and planners beautiful works of art. They invite their creativity into the administration of their lives. Others develop reward systems, making time spent with creativity a prize: "Once I've filed my taxes, I get to paint/bake/go dancing." I personally like to engage my creativity while I'm cleaning, walking the dog, or cooking by daydreaming about ideas I'll write later, or listening to podcasts that help me broaden my approach to creative work.

As you find ways of integrating your creative and practical lives, you'll naturally start to find your own rhythm—a way of being present with your creativity and engaging with your daily life at the same time. It won't always be easy; our juggling hero can't control whether a sea breeze sweeps through and knocks the pentacles out of their hands. But it will become second nature.

When the Two of Pentacles appears, take it as a sign to reflect on how you're feeling about the balance of your creativity and daily life, and brainstorm a few ways that integration could feel smoother for you.

Creative Prompts for the Two of Pentacles

Make a collage inspired by all the things you feel you have to balance in your creative life. Let this be a cathartic moment of realizing just how much you're juggling and a reminder that it's OK to find it challenging sometimes.

Write a story or short film that stars a juggler.

Pick your favorite detail in this card and create a piece of art inspired by it. (That ridiculous hat better be a strong contender.)

Journal about the strategies you already have in place to create balance in your creative life, and come up with a few additional strategies you could try out.

The Two of Pentacles Spread

This spread can help you reflect on the sense of balance you're experiencing in your creative life right now. It's great for those moments when you feel off-kilter, but also perfect for checking in with yourself regularly.

Shuffle your deck. Draw the card off the top, the card off the bottom, and a card from the middle of the deck and lay all three down in the spread that follows. Then reflect on how the cards you draw relate to the prompts in the spread.

··✳ 1 ✳··

Where do I need to find balance in my creative life right now?

··✳ 2 ✳··

Where am I already achieving balance in my creative life?

··✳ 3 ✳··

What small act will help me maintain or create better balance?

Create in Community

with the
Three of Pentacles

Creativity can often feel like a siloed act. In many cases, it *is* something that you foster on your own. But that doesn't mean that creativity exists in a completely solitary vacuum. More often than not, at some point in your creative journey, you'll need the help, support, and collaboration of others to bring your vision to life.

The Three of Pentacles is a card that captures the spirit of teamwork and nods at what can be achieved when creatives bring their skills together in the service of a larger goal.

In the card's illustration, a craftsperson puts the finishing touches on a cathedral, while an architect and a monk look on, conferring over the building plan. This is a team at work, each bringing their unique expertise and point of view to the table to ensure that the final result is the best it can be. This is creativity in community.

Plenty of creative disciplines are naturally collaborative and require a community spirit to bring a project to life—plays and films need directors, actors, designers, writers, cinematographers, and stage managers; musical acts often require multiple musicians, sound engineers, tour managers, and technicians. Most dancers work with partners and choreographers; professional photographers work with models and lighting experts; and creative businesses rely on quick-thinking teams that can generate and action ideas, whether that means coding a new app, designing a new product, developing a new ad campaign, or coming up with a business strategy.

Even the less obviously collaborative creative pursuits—poetry, painting, vlogging, you name it—benefit from bringing a collaborative spirit to the work. Editors, curators, fellow content creators, and clients can all be valuable teammates in your creative undertakings.

Teamwork Really Does Make the Dream Work

The Three of Pentacles celebrates the teamwork at play in creative projects. It reminds you that needing help and support in your creative work is completely normal.

Elsewhere in this book, the Two of Cups invites you to reflect on and recognize the *emotional* benefits of having support and meaningful creative partnerships. Now, the Three of Pentacles highlights the *material* benefits of teamwork. Collaboration doesn't just feel good; it generates a solid foundation for your creative success.

Building community as part of your creative process is an important step in realizing your most ambitious and exciting creative ideas. No cathedral comes together through the work of one person, so if you want to create lasting work, you'll need teammates on your side.

When this card comes up in a reading, consider it a prompt to ask for the help you need in your creative life, to acknowledge the support you already have, and to foster an overall appreciation of the role community plays in your creative pursuits.

Creative Prompts for the Three of Pentacles

Invite friends and peers to make a version of this card (or an artwork inspired by this card) in community with you.

Write a short script inspired by this card and cast friends and family in the roles. Then film the piece or perform it for an audience.

Design bespoke tarot cards to represent people whom you consider to be part of your team.

Journal about your experiences with creating in community in the past. How have these experiences enriched your creative life? How would you like to improve upon them in the future?

The Three of Pentacles Spread

Ready to build up your creative community? Turn to this spread to help you figure out what you're looking for.

Shuffle your deck three times, then divide it into three piles. Choose one card off the top of each pile and lay them out in the spread that follows. Then reflect on how the cards you draw relate to the prompts in the spread.

·* 1 *·
How can I benefit from building a creative team around me?

·* 2 *·
What quality do I need to look for in creative teammates?

·* 3 *·
What quality should I avoid in creative teammates?

Respect Your Limits

with the

IV

Four of
Pentacles

The Four of Pentacles is a card about recognizing your limits and acknowledging when you've hit them. In doing that work, you can invest more thoughtfully in the creative pursuits that matter most to you, instead of spreading yourself too thin by saying yes to absolutely everything.

The card's illustration presents a figure who is completely incapacitated by the scope of what they have taken on. Their hands are wrapped tightly around a pentacle, their feet must stay planted on the ground to pin down the pentacles beneath them, and there's even a fourth pentacle balanced on their head. It's not just that they are overburdened; they are *clinging* to their burdens, unwilling to loosen their grip or relax their posture. This figure is trying to keep so many things under their control that they cannot physically move for risk of losing what they are holding on to.

It's not a very subtle metaphor, is it?

Free Yourself Up

If you struggle with setting boundaries and often find yourself overcommitted and low on energy and resources, or if you feel like you have to court burnout in an effort to prove your worth, then the imagery in the Four of Pentacles may feel uncomfortably close to home for you. And you're not alone.

Many modern creatives see themselves in the Four of Pentacles—overstretched and desperately putting themselves under pressure to find a way to make it all work. This card can act as a mirror, reflecting the ways in which you're doing yourself a disservice by trying to do it all, even though you don't have the capacity. The card can offer the tough love you need to acknowledge that you simply don't have enough arms and legs to spin all the plates you're trying to keep spinning in the air.

Grappling with the fact that you've taken on too much is hard, thankless work. It gets worse before it gets better. But it's crucial to sustaining a creative life. You cannot move forward creatively from a Four of Pentacles position. You can only stay still, exhausted and trapped by the balancing act.

When this card comes up for you, let it be the invitation you need to free up your hands. Allow some opportunities to pass through them, so that you are not constantly overextended and overstimulated. See it as a reminder to respect your limits and boundaries instead of constantly testing them.

Creative Prompts for the Four of Pentacles

Imagine what the central figure might be doing if they weren't weighed down by obligation. Write a story or paint a picture based on the freer life you've dreamed up for the character in this card.

Create a self-portrait that imagines you as the Four of Pentacles character. Get creative with how you illustrate the pentacles—imagine how they can represent things you're holding on to even when they're not healthy for you.

Make a list of the obligations that are weighing you down right now and strategize with a friend, partner, or mentor about how you can lighten your load.

Journal about a time you felt peak Four of Pentacles energy. What happened, and how did you ultimately solve the problem of being too weighed down to move?

The Four of Pentacles Spread

It's not always easy to see when you've hit your limits, or to decide how to lighten your load—let this spread guide you through that process so you can return to your life and your creative work a little freer.

Take a deep breath while shuffling your cards. On the exhale, draw four cards and lay them down in the spread that follows. Then, reflect on how the cards you draw relate to the prompts in the spread.

··• 1 •··

Where am I struggling in my creative life right now?

··✻ 2 •··

What obligations are contributing to my struggle?

··✻ 3 •··

How are these obligations holding me back from creative satisfaction?

··• 4 •··

How can I be better at respecting my own limits and protecting my freedom?

Hold Space for the

Hard Stuff

with the Five of Pentacles

Creativity does not always feel productive. In fact, pursuing your creative goals can sometimes be a slog—creativity can ask a lot of your energy, time, and other resources. Some creative challenges take more than they give, and that can be draining.

Featuring two completely worn-out, injured figures struggling through the snow, the Five of Pentacles can hold space for the difficult parts of your creative journey: the idea that just won't come together, the piece of work that just won't sell, even the tarot reading you just can't make sense of. This image acknowledges your experience: Yes, this is a hard moment. You're not crazy. You're not weak. You're just a human dealing with difficulty right now, and you deserve the time and space to recover.

The figures in the card are not prepared to keep pushing forward—they are wet, cold, hurt, barefoot. They cannot be forced to keep moving toward their destination. Instead, they need a moment of comfort, a break on the road. A chance to warm up, restock their supplies, and treat their most urgent wounds. They need kindness and hospitality, a safe space. If this card comes up for you, you might need to offer yourself the same thing.

Come In from the Cold

When you first take in this card, you may only notice the biting cold, the weakened characters, the bracing wind, and feel a sense of hopelessness. If you're having a Five of Pentacles moment in your life, you may wonder: Will this ever get any better?

The good news is that despite this card's grim initial impression, hope floats in the background, right within reach. Just behind the weary travelers is the stained-glass window of a church, representing solace, retreat, and community care. It turns out these travelers aren't on an endless journey through the cold—they are finally reaching a well-deserved and much-needed place of shelter. Just a few more steps and they can come in from the cold, be fed, warmed, and cared for.

This is a card about advocating for your needs and making pit stops to take care of yourself when you're in a tricky period on your creative journey. You can't keep fighting the good fight if you're worn down and out of resources.

When this card appears, focus on giving yourself the safe refuge you deserve. Validate your feelings of hardship, and offer yourself a break from the thankless work that's been wearing you down. Look to your community for extra support, and give yourself full permission to tend to your physical and emotional needs, so that once you've recovered, you're ready to face the elements again.

Creative Prompts for the Five of Pentacles

Use snow as a motif in a piece of creative work, in whatever creative medium feels right for you.

Design a modern version of this card. What kind of hard terrain might the characters be walking through, and what kind of solace might be waiting around the corner for them?

Build yourself a first aid kit for creative burnout. Put your favorite tea and treats inside, but also include things that make you feel connected to your creativity, like dried flowers in your favorite color, a postcard of your favorite painting, or the lyrics of your favorite song.

Journal about what you feel when you look at the Five of Pentacles. How does it challenge you, and how does it give you comfort? What questions does it prompt you to ask yourself, and how does it reflect your creative journey now?

The Five of Pentacles Spread

Use this spread when you're facing hard times in your creative life—the cards you draw can hold space for your struggle and help you seek out solace.

Shuffle your deck and lay three cards out in the spread that follows. Then reflect on how the cards you draw relate to the prompts in the spread.

·◦✷ 1 ✷◦·

What creative hardship am I facing?

·◦✷ 2 ✷◦·

Where can I seek out solace on my creative journey?

·◦✷ 3 ✷◦·

How can my community support me right now?

Creative Support

Give and Accept

with the Six of Pentacles

The theme of the Six of Pentacles is give and take. It illustrates a scene between three figures: two beggars kneel before a character who's better dressed and in better health. The standing figure holds a scale in one hand and drops pentacles into the open hands of the figure on their right. Whether or not there's anything to spare for the second beggar is open for interpretation.

Because the Pentacles are associated with earthly resources, the card can be an invitation to examine how you're using, sharing, or seeking resources in your life. It's about recognizing where you can make contributions and where you may be in need of the generosity of others.

When it comes to your creative life, see this card as an opportunity to reflect on how you're giving and taking on your creative journey. How can you offer support, and where do you need it?

Explore Your Gifts and Your Needs

This is one of those cards where it can be helpful to check in on what stands out most to you in the image. Do you relate to the figure holding the scales or one of the beggars? The card has been traditionally associated with "success"—an interpretation that centers on the charitable figure. If you find yourself most drawn to this central figure, consider the ways in which you share your successes with others. How do you give back, hold space, and lift others up when you're in the position to do so? What do you have to offer your wider creative community—skills and guidance, financial support, or other resources?

Think, too, about how giving back or offering what you have can be a creatively satisfying act in and of itself.

On the flip side, if one of the kneeling figures aligns more closely to your current creative experience, then you need to focus less on what you have to give and more on what resources and support you need. It's a prompt to put pride aside and ask for help, whether that's seeking funding for a project, taking lessons in a new skill, asking for client introductions, or identifying other resources that people in your network may be able to provide.

When the card appears, remember that you might be simultaneously rich in some areas and poor in others—take the opportunity to explore both sides of yourself, and consider how you can both be generous and seek out generosity at the same time.

Creative Prompts for the Six of Pentacles

Script a short film or comic strip that gives more insight into the wider story of this card. Who is each character, what do they want and need, and what do they have to offer? What might surprise an audience about each one?

Offer your creative skills to a friend, family member, or colleague who you know could use the help.

Reach out to a friend or mentor who can help you develop a creative skill or access another resource. If you're not ready for this yet, spend some time brainstorming about where you feel you need to grow in your creative life and who might be poised to help you.

Journal about which character in this card you relate to the most and why. What does this affinity tell you about your current creative experience?

The Six of Pentacles Spread

This spread can help you reflect on what you have to offer and what you want to gain in your creative life. Use it regularly to check in on how you're doing, what you need, and where you can give back to your community.

Shuffle your deck and flip through until you find the Six of Pentacles. Draw the two cards behind the Six and lay them down in the first two positions of the spread. Then reshuffle and repeat for spread positions three and four. Once all the cards are down, reflect on how the cards you draw relate to the prompts in the spread.

·❋ 1 ❋· What resource can I share?

·❋ 2 ❋· How can I share that resource?

·❋ 3 ❋· What creative resource do I need to help me to grow?

·❋ 4 ❋· Where can I look for help?

Pause and Reflect

VII

with
the

Seven of
Pentacles

Creative work can often be all go with no stops, and many creative minds thrive on that fast-paced energy. But if the Seven of Pentacles has come to the fore for you, you're being encouraged to slow down for a minute. Not so much because you need to rest, but because you need to do the important work of taking stock of where you're at, what you've done so far, and what this means going forward.

This card doesn't want you to stop and smell the roses for the sake of it (though there are plenty of cards in the tarot that do!). Rather, the Seven of Pentacles wants you to be shrewd—to cast an expert eye over everything you've achieved up until now, then use those observations to calculate how far you've still got to go, and what you're going to need to get there.

In the card, a gardener stands still, surveying their crop. The character is taking stock of what their work is yielding (seven pentacles so far). They're proud of what they've achieved so far, but they know they're not done yet. They've still got their tool in hand, and their posture isn't fully relaxed, almost as if they plan to go right back to work once this moment of reflection comes to an end.

Get the Lay of the Land

Busy creatives can learn a lot from the Seven of Pentacles gardener; this figure knows it's important to hustle and get results, but they also have no qualms stepping back and surveying the lay of the land.

This coolheaded, strategic approach is particularly important to practice if you're heading up a creative business or working on a long-term project like an album, novel, or feature film.

Projects with big scopes require moments of pause and reflection, even if it's tempting to hurdle blindly toward the finish line. Taking that time to review what you've done and reflect on what's working can help you course correct before any potential issues become unmanageable, and it can also help you assess where you might need additional resources and support to make your way to the end.

Alongside offering an opportunity for damage control, this card can also be a huge treat for your creative soul. It's a reminder that you don't need to cross the finish line to marvel at your accomplishments. It's an encouragement to stop and pat yourself on the back along the way. Whenever you draw it, take a moment to tell yourself how proud you are of what you've achieved so far. Then ask yourself: How can I keep this momentum going?

Creative Prompts for the Seven of Pentacles

Plant your own small seed and nurture it to flowering over time. Check in with every stage of the growth process; take the time to reflect on what your plant needs from you and how you can meet that need.

Reimagine the pentacles in this card as rich, colorful flowers. Create a piece of visual art that captures the flowers in all their full beauty.

Visit a local botanical garden or park and spend some time taking in what's growing there. Bonus points for bringing a sketchbook, notebook, or camera and turning what you see into art.

Journal about where you're at in your creative journey at the moment. What have you nurtured into being, and what progress do you still want to make?

The Seven of Pentacles Spread

Taking the time to reflect and review can help you bring your creative projects to life. Turn to this card anytime you need help slowing down and observing your progress.

Shuffle your deck seven times, then draw three cards and lay them out in the spread that follows. Take a moment to observe the three cards before you reflect on how the cards you draw relate to the prompts in the spread.

··✴ 1 ✴··

What's going well in this project so far?

··✴ 2 ✴··

Where do I want to make improvements?

··✴ 3 ✴··

What can help me keep growing?

Hone Your Craft

with the

VIII

Eight of
Pentacles

In the Eight of Pentacles, a craftsperson is hard at work engraving pentacles, one after the other after the other. You're watching the central figure refine their process and hone their craft one pentacle at a time.

For creatives, this card is crucial. Its emphasis on process and practice is so deeply important for anyone who wants to live a sustainable creative life.

Practice may not always be the sexiest aspect of creativity. Many of us love the high of living in the more elusive, ephemeral state of "accidental" creativity; we relish the feeling of striking gold without having labored over the process. But you're more likely to have accidental gold moments if you introduce some discipline into your creative practice.

Center the Process

If the word "discipline" made you cringe to read, don't worry—it made me cringe to write it, too.

I don't like the association the word has with punishment and perfection, but part of this card's job is to help you divorce the negative connotations of discipline and instead recognize that you can find a creative regimen that supports and uplifts your practice.

Notice that there's only one character in the card: the artisan, diligently at work. There's no boss breathing down their neck, no ticking clock, no pressure, no stress. You're not looking at a productive machine, but simply a human being dedicated to improving their work.

The card makes no promises about outcome; it's not assurance that "practice makes perfect." Instead, it centers on the process, the meditative quality of making progress for your own satisfaction, a goal that creatives often lose sight of when they share or monetize their work.

There's so much beauty in coming back to the work itself. In sitting with yourself, putting down one stitch, one brushstroke, one word, over and over just to see what you're capable of.

Whenever the Eight of Pentacles appears, it's a call to ground yourself in process and practice. To find joy in the doing of creative work, in stretching your muscles, testing your limits, making discoveries as you go. Don't expect practice to make perfect, but trust that practice is the prayer you make to your creativity, the communion that connects you with the magic you're craving; let yourself be amazed by what happens when you give yourself the time and space to keep working.

Creative Prompts for the Eight of Pentacles

Write a haiku inspired by this card. Then, rewrite that haiku seven times. See what happens when you intentionally set out to hone your craft and your message.

Join a coworking group focused on your artistic medium. There are many communities you can show up to (online or in person). Groups where you write, knit, or craft in community—silently, but together— are hugely popular, and so are more social open mics and jam sessions for comedians and musicians. If you can't find what you're looking for, start your own group committed to facilitating practice and process.

Decorate (or redecorate) a dedicated "practice space" in your home. Make it a place you want to spend time in, and let yourself be enticed to show up and work on your craft.

Journal about your relationship to practice and process. When do you practice your craft? When and why do you avoid practice? How can the Eight of Pentacles help you reframe your relationship with practice?

The Eight of Pentacles Spread

Practice may not make perfect, but practice is always the perfect way to engage your creativity. Use this spread whenever you need some support in recommitting to your craft.

Shuffle your deck and flip through until you find the Eight of Pentacles, then draw out the two cards directly behind it. Reflect on how the cards you draw relate to the prompts in the spread.

··✳ 1 ✳··

How can I support myself to practice my craft?

··✳ 2 ✳··

What kind of benefits will practice have on my creativity?

Invest in Yourself

with the

IX

Nine of Pentacles

The Nine of Pentacles has traditionally been the patron card of independent business-people. The figure poised in their luxurious garden, surrounded by pentacles, represents a vision for success that many business owners aspire to: Here is someone who has managed to create enough security for themselves that they have time to appreciate their life.

You don't have to monetize your creativity to benefit from this card's wisdom. Because no matter what your creative goals are, the Nine of Pentacles simply wants you to give your creative pursuits everything you can, to invest in the creative life you deserve, and to enjoy the rewards of that investment.

(Investment, by the way, doesn't have to mean pouring money into your creative pursuits. Your time, energy, and commitment are equally valuable capital. In fact, if you *are* going to invest money in your creative work, it's wise to ensure you're able to invest those other things first.)

Creative Investment Is a Long Game

Investing in your creativity will look different depending on where you're at in your creative journey, what's going on in the rest of your life, what your creative goals are, and what resources are realistically available to you. The best investments are prudent and made with long-term stability and security in mind.

You don't need to stockpile everything you have and mainline every resource into your creative pursuits. You must simply recognize your creative goals as worthy of investment, even if what you've got to put into the pot feels meager.

Right now, you might be able to afford twenty minutes every other day to work on a project. Somewhere down the line, you may invest time, money, and energy on a weeklong creative retreat. You might invest your efforts in helping out a fellow creative who you know can support you in the future, or you might invest in months' worth of research into preparing for a project you want to tackle. These are all valid ways of investing in your creative journey, and all of them will come with their own unique reward.

Like most of the advice in the suit of Pentacles, this card wants you to remember that creative growth is a long game, and you do need some strategy if you want to keep playing. While it's important to entertain your sparks and pursue your ideas passionately, it's equally vital to be able to ration and invest your creative energy and resources thoughtfully.

Creative Prompts for the Nine of Pentacles

Develop a "creative budget" for yourself. Be honest and realistic about how much time, energy, and money you have to invest in your creativity for the next month, and make a plan that honors what you actually have to give.

Make a list of three ways you are currently investing in your creativity (hint: working with this book is one of them!), and set aside time to daydream about the reward waiting for you at the end.

Write a story about a character who invests in an unconventional stock. Draw another tarot card to indicate whether this decision goes well or poorly for them, and then finish the story accordingly.

Journal about the ways you've invested in your creativity in the past. What rewards have you enjoyed as a result of those investments? Where could your investment strategy stand to improve?

The Nine of Pentacles Spread

This spread can help you reflect on where and how you want to invest in your creativity, as well as give you the chance to see what current creative investments are already paying off for you.

Shuffle your deck nine times. Then, spread your cards out face down on the table and intentionally select three cards. Lay those cards out, face up, in the spread that follows and reflect on how the cards you draw relate to the prompts in the spread.

```
          ··✳ 1 ✳··

          How can I
          invest in my
          creativity
          right now?


  ··✳ 2 ✳··              ··✳ 3 ✳··

  How can this           How am
  investment in          I already
  my creativity          experiencing a
  reward me in           return on the
  the long run?          investments
                         I've made in
                         my creativity?
```

Appreciate Every Creative Day

X

with the Ten of Pentacles

If you're reading this, all you need in this moment is to live your creative life. Minute by minute, step by step, piece by piece, appreciate just how wonderful and magical it is to walk through this world as a creative person. You need to acknowledge that even if all you're doing is walking through the world, you *are* a creative person.

The card itself is busy, especially when you work with the classic Waite-Smith version, which is particularly packed with details. It depicts a market scene, full to the brim with all kinds of characters and small moments. An elder feeds their dogs in the front left corner; a parent and child walk beneath the arch of a bridge; and another figure walks in the opposite direction. Through the arch, you can glimpse clear blue skies, a tower, and the countryside in the distance. In Pamela Colman Smith's original illustrations, placards adorned the stone arches, illustrating the wider world of the tarot and beyond—a set of scales, a cliffside, a moated fortress.

There's too much going on in this card for it to be about any one thing. Instead, it manages, somehow, to be about everything.

Living Is a Creative Act

Visually, everything in this card is connected—all the human characters are in contact somehow. The two standing adults' shoulders brush; the child strokes one of the dogs, while the other dog sits with their snout resting on their master's knee.

It might represent a life cycle, or the connectedness of all things, but it can also simply illustrate the richly woven tapestry of everyday life. There's so much opportunity for story here, so much potential to flesh out every little moment into a world of its own.

The moments of your life are the same. Every millisecond is worth cherishing. And in cherishing those moments, in being alive and present, you are living creatively.

Many cards in this suit are concerned with how you use, preserve, and share resources—your time, energy, money, attention—in ways that benefit your creativity. This card is here to remind you that the pure and simple act of living is a creative resource all its own.

Sure, some days are for buckling down and making things. Some days are for celebrating what you've already made. But some days are just for living, and those days are essential.

Whenever this card comes up for you, remember that every day is a thread in the rich tapestry of your creative life. Don't take any of them for granted.

Creative Prompts for the Ten of Pentacles

Design a collage, tapestry, or puzzle that turns the magic of your daily life into art.

Split this image up into multiple frames and tell each tiny story present in the image through the medium of a comic strip or graphic story.

Craft a poem, song, or work of visual art that honors this exact moment in your creative life.

Journal about the everyday moments in your life that are actually quite magical. Write about each one you can think of in detail.

The Ten of Pentacles Spread

This spread is designed to help you find and appreciate the magic in your everyday life, even if it doesn't feel obvious.

Shuffle your deck with your eyes closed. Shuffle while you tune in to your breath and the space around you, feeling the connection between the breath you draw in and the breath you put back out into the world. When you're ready, draw three cards from the deck and lay them out in the spread that follows. Then reflect on how the cards you draw relate to the prompts in the spread.

··✳ 1 ✳··

Where can I find creative magic in my everyday life?

··✳ 2 ✳··

Where *else* can I find creative magic in my everyday life?

··✳ 3 ✳··

Where *else* can I find creative magic in my everyday life?

Embrace Ambition

with the

Page of Pentacles

All the Pages in the tarot represent facets of curiosity, one of the most important traits for living a creative life. The Page of Cups is open to being playful with whatever comes their way; the Page of Swords gives everything a try even when they feel clueless; and the Page of Wands showers everything in their path with deep attention. But the Page of Pentacles unlocks a new point of view: Curiosity is more than a whim—it's a resource. One that, managed well, can take you and your creativity to new heights.

This Page has traditionally been seen as a scholar, someone dedicated to growing their knowledge. You can see it in the way they hold their coin up to the light, making a study of it.

This card positions knowledge as a resource and well-placed curiosity as the key to unlocking and growing that resource.

What's Your Agenda?

The Page of Pentacles doesn't simply love learning—no, this Page loves what learning affords them. They understand that knowledge can level up their skills and give them a competitive edge. Curiosity isn't just a flight of fancy; when curiosity leads to serious study, it opens a door into sharper skills and sweeter opportunities.

The fact that you're reading this book probably means you've got some Page of Pentacles energy in you. On some level, you understand that making a study of something can help you develop new resources and tools for getting where you need to go. You picked this book up because you were curious, but your curiosity has a clear agenda: You want to be more creative, understand the tarot better, or both.

The ambition to learn and improve sometimes comes with sharp edges. Modern society has a tendency to wag its fingers at people (especially femme-presenting folks or people of color) it deems "too ambitious." But the Page of Pentacles is here to remind you that your desire to improve, grow, and take your creative ambitions as far as you can go is golden, and you are allowed to pursue those ambitions. You deserve the resource of knowledge, and you deserve to use that resource to live your best life.

When this card appears, make an effort to learn something new. Take a class, pick up a book on a subject you're curious about, or ask a friend to teach you a new skill. By all means, enjoy the process for the sake of learning, but recognize, too, that you're making a meaningful investment in yourself and your creativity.

Creative Prompts for the Page of Pentacles

Write an essay, or record a vlog, about a time you dedicated yourself to learning something unconventional. Share your knowledge and how the experience changed your perspective and helped you grow.

Make a list of things you'd like to learn and consider the ways each thing could benefit your creative experience, process, and skills.

Sign up for a class, or do a skills exchange with a friend, with the intention of upskilling your creative work.

Journal about your relationship with ambition. When have your ambitions been supported, and when have you been made to feel bad about them? What have those experiences taught you, and how do you want to embrace your ambition going forward?

The Page of Pentacles Spread

If you're ready to embrace your creative ambition and put your curiosity to work toward gaining helpful knowledge, turn to this simple but effective spread.

You have a choice when using this spread: You can either draw a random card for the first card position, to represent your creative ambition, or you can intentionally choose a card that you feel best represents that ambition. Once you've made your decision and laid the first card down, shuffle your deck and draw a card to place in the second spread position. Then, reflect on how the cards you've laid out relate to the prompts in the spread.

```
┌─────────────┐  ┌─────────────┐
│  ·*· 1 ·*·  │  │  ·* 2 *·    │
│             │  │             │
│             │  │             │
│   What is   │  │   What can I│
│ my creative │  │ learn to help│
│  ambition?  │  │  me achieve │
│             │  │that ambition?│
│             │  │             │
└─────────────┘  └─────────────┘
```

Trust Your Creative Worth

Worth

with

the

Knight of Pentacles

The Pentacles are thematically tied to your resources (time, money, energy, skills, attention, etc.), and they prompt you to explore the value you assign to said resources and to your creativity in general.

The Knight of Pentacles is the ultimate defender of your value. It's a call to stand up for what you bring to the table and to honor that value whenever you share your creative resources.

Other cards in this suit have touched on this theme, too—notably the Six and the Nine—but the Knight takes it even further.

This card wants you to show up to every interaction with a deep-seated understanding of just how much value you're bringing to the table.

Stand Your Own Ground

Many creatives devalue themselves on a regular basis. It's often not our fault. We live in a culture that regularly dismisses the value of creativity. Funding for the arts is the first thing to go when institutions cut budgets; the majority of professional creatives are underpaid and overworked (minus the handful who scrape through to the top); and no field has been under more constant scrutiny in the age of AI.

We're told to be grateful for scraps, not to waste time monetizing our creative work, that anyone can write an email or design a logo, that every striving artist needs a "backup plan."

No wonder we question our value and all too often leap at opportunities designed to exploit our unique skills, talents, and passions. (Raise your hand if you've ever been asked to do unpaid work in exchange for "exposure.") But the Knight of Pentacles won't stand for this.

This card demands you stand your ground and recognize your creativity as something you should only give away on your own terms. The Knight offers up their pentacle with a relaxed but obvious confidence. Even their horse stands firm and steady, all four hooves planted firmly on the ground.

When this card comes up, take it as a sign to hold your ground and honor your own worth: You don't need to sacrifice the value of your creative work for anyone or anything—not for money, not for love, and definitely not for exposure. If you're struggling to see the value in your own creative process or work, let this Knight come to your rescue and remind you that your creativity matters and that you deserve to set the terms of the offer when you're giving your work away.

Creative Prompts for the Knight of Pentacles

Write a short story or film about a character who gives up their most cherished possession to someone who doesn't value it. What happens next? Do they get it back, or do they have to learn to live with what they have done?

Make a price list for your creativity, but be playful about it. Instead of assigning monetary value, take some creative license. A cake baked by you is worth two hundred flutters of a butterfly's wing; you will knit a friend a scarf in exchange for unlimited pickups at the airport; and so on.

Share something of high creative value with someone you love and no one else. Note how it feels to take charge of whom you give your creative resources to.

Journal about moments when you've felt externally valued versus moments when you've valued yourself. What differentiated the two, and which turned out better in the long run?

The Knight of Pentacles Spread

Turn to this spread for a pick-me-up and some practical advice on communicating and protecting your value.

Shuffle your deck and draw four cards. Lay them face down on the table in the spread that follows, then turn them over one by one, so that you can take in the message of each card on its own. Then, reflect on how the cards you draw relate to the prompts in the spread.

·⁕ 1 ⁕·	·⁕ 2 ⁕·	·⁕ 3 ⁕·	·⁕ 4 ⁕·
What do I deeply value in my creative life?	What could I value more in my creative life?	How can I communicate my creative value to others?	How can I protect my creative value from anyone who would take advantage of it?

Ground Yourself

with the

King of
Pentacles

All of the tarot suits are largely concerned with movement. The Cups explore how your emotions flow through you; the Swords reflect on how your thoughts move you and impact your actions; the Wands draw attention to the passions and visions you chase; and the Pentacles are metaphors for the way you grow and build your resources. But within each suit are moments of stillness, and the King of Pentacles offers one of the tarot's most powerful examples of how stillness can be an asset, a flex, a magic trick just as impactful as the action-packed cards that surround it.

In Pamela Colman Smith's 1909 illustration of this card, the King of Pentacles has become one with the earth. The grapevines that decorate their robes are indistinguishable from the real vines growing up around them. There are vines spilling out from the King's boots, hanging over their shoulders, nestled into their crown. There's no telling where the King stops and nature begins.

The other key symbol in this card is the King's throne of bulls. The bulls are linked to the astrological symbol Taurus, an earth sign that's known for moving slowly and deliberately; they also stand for the King's determination to protect their own peace.

Don't Be Swayed

This image captures a person who is deeply committed to their own sense of identity, values, and stability. The King of Pentacles cannot be swayed. And in fast-paced creative environments, this sense of grounded conviction can be a superpower.

When you're creatively grounded, you are unflappable. No mere inconvenience or distraction can rip you up by your roots. You know that things may come and go—ideas, opportunities, collaborators, successes, entire careers—but you and your creativity will keep on going and growing together.

It's not easily achieved, but the King of Pentacles is challenging you to try to find your values, your peace, and root into them. Don't let yourself be swayed by outside forces or overwhelmed by the rat race. Trust that if you plant yourself in the solid, fertile ground of your own self-knowledge, then you, and everything around you, are going to grow lush and beautiful.

Creative Prompts for the King of Pentacles

Try a grounding meditation. Close your eyes and plant your feet on the floor if you can. Connect to your breath and imagine that you are breathing in through the crown of your head. Move your attention down: Breathe in through your forehead, your eyelids, your cheeks. Move your attention down your body in small increments, breathing into each individual part of your body one at a time. When you finally get to your feet, imagine that when you exhale, roots grow out of your feet and connect you to the floor. Inhale into the floor a couple of times and then, on your final exhale, let the air move back up through your body as you breathe out, and imagine the breath blooming out of your head. Do this a couple of times, inhaling in through your imagined roots and out through the imagined blossom at the crown of your head.

Create a piece of art inspired by your favorite aspect of this card.

Find a Taurus horoscope for today and write a short story, comic, or film script based on what the horoscope says.

Journal about what being creatively rooted means to you. How have you achieved it, and in what ways do you want to keep working toward it? How does the King of Pentacles inspire you to ground yourself?

The King of Pentacles Spread

To help you find an unflappable, unshakable sense of peace and groundedness in your creative life, turn to this spread.

First, move through the grounding meditation suggested in the creative prompts for this card, shuffling while you complete the exercise. Then, draw three cards and lay them out in the spread that follows. Reflect on how the cards you draw relate to the prompts in the spread.

·*1*·
How can I ground myself in my creativity?

·*2*·
How can I protect my peace?

·*3*·
Where in my creative life is stillness most powerful?

Come Home to Your Creativity

with
the
Queen of
Pentacles

As the final card entry in this book, the Queen of Pentacles has played their part perfectly, waiting to offer you the most quintessential advice the tarot has for engaging with your creativity: Stick around, give it time, and always, always come back, no matter how far you go or how long you're away.

This card is all about patience and the gentle but impossibly strong act of giving yourself the time, respect, and unerring faithfulness you need to build your creative life. Because the creative life you're dreaming of, and moving toward, won't happen overnight.

Sure, there will be bolts of creative lightning that illuminate your practice for days, weeks, sometimes even years at a time (see the entire suit of Wands for proof); there will be sudden shifts in mindset that herald bold new creative eras (aka, Swords moments); and there will be an ocean of feelings you might sink into at any moment, for better or worse (hello, Cups). It's easy to get caught up in all that action and forget that at the end of the day, all roads lead back to you. It's completely within your power to build a creative home that's greater than the sum of all your feelings, thoughts, and passions. Something that lasts, even when the feelings and the thoughts and the passions fade.

Throughout all of those wild rides, you can rely on Pentacles energy to help you tend to the foundations and use the resources at your disposal to build a safe, secure place for your creativity to come home to. A place where it—and you—can always flourish.

Keep the Porch Light On

The Queen of Pentacles is the ultimate empty nester. You and your creativity are always flying the coop, heading off on adventures, leaving them behind. And yet, the Queen—your deepest creative foundation—trusts you will always come back home. They leave a light on for you, and you're always welcome at their table.

But that sense of security can only be there for you to come home to if you raise it up first. If you have the faith to show up and plant the seeds so that one day, when you leave the nest, you won't forget where home is.

When this card appears, remember that you can always come home to your creativity. Your creative life is yours to nurture, protect, and cherish. Find that light, turn it on, and know it's always there, guiding you even in the middle of the night.

At the risk of sounding like an absolute cliché, it's true what they say: Home really is where the heart is, and if your creative life is being lived from the heart, then you are always home.

And if you find yourself away from that home without knowing how to get back, I happen to know of a little map with seventy-eight stops, one you can carry around in your pocket so that you'll always have a piece of your creative home . . . and a handful of breadcrumbs to lead you back to it.

Creative Prompts for the Queen of Pentacles

Design the creative home of your dreams. Feel free to take this prompt as literally or figuratively as you see fit.

Write a story or script about someone who waits for something forever. Leave the ending ambiguous. How will you balance the hope and the melancholy of the theme?

Design a version of the Queen of Pentacles that you can display in your home, to remind yourself that your creative life is an important part of your sense of home.

Journal about what feeling at home in your creativity means to you. How has your relationship with the tarot deepened that sense of home?

The Queen of Pentacles Spread

No matter where you are on your creative journey, let this spread hold you in its loving arms.

Close your eyes and shuffle, imagining yourself in the comfiest, homiest situation possible. When you're ready, open your eyes and draw three cards. Lay them out face up in the spread that follows, then reflect on how the cards you draw relate to the prompts in the spread.

·⁎ 1 ⁎·

What does my creative home feel like?

·⁎ 2 ⁎·

How can I come back home to my creativity when I've been away?

·⁎ 3 ⁎·

How can I carry my creative home with me wherever I go?

PENTACLES EXERCISES

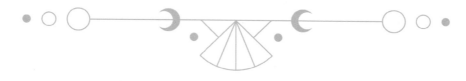

Exercise 1

Separate your deck out so that you have a stack for every suit and the Major Arcana (you can put the Majors aside for this exercise). Shuffle the Pentacles and draw a card. Then draw that card's equivalent from every other suit pile (i.e., if you draw an Eight of Pentacles, draw the Eight of Cups, Swords, and Wands). Write a story based on these four cards.

Exercise 2

Build yourself a "Bank of Creativity," aka a piggy bank or savings pot where the funds inside must be used for creative endeavors. Aim to put a small amount into the pot every month. When the time feels right, draw a Pentacle card to help you decide how to spend the cash.

Exercise 3

The Pentacles are associated with the element of earth. Lay out all fourteen cards and map each card to a season that the Earth moves through over the course of the year. How does seeing the suit this way affect your perception of the cards?

Exercise 4

Flip through all fourteen Pentacle cards, really taking in each one before choosing your favorite. Imagine a fictional person who exemplifies everything you like about this card, and write a poem, love song, or short story about them.

Sample Reading for Creativity

Here's how I might read a tarot spread in a creative context.

For this example, I'll be using the Sun Spread from page 83, which is all about giving me the tools to believe my own hype and shine a light on me and my creativity.

··✷ 2 ✷··

What specific achievement should I shout more proudly about?

··✷ 1 ✷··

Where can I give myself more credit?

··✷ 3 ✷··

What is an affirmation I can use when I'm not feeling my own light?

Before I start reading a spread, there are two things I like to do.

First, I set an intention out loud. For this spread, I hold my deck in my hands, telling it (and myself): "I am drawing cards to help me recognize the light that my creativity brings to the world."

Second, I make some broad notes about the spread before I pull cards. In this case, I note down my intuitive answers to each prompt. *Where can I give myself more credit?* I make a note that I think I need to give myself more credit for my creative resilience—over the last year I've had a lot of setbacks, and I've often felt like they've torn me down. But the truth is I'm still here, writing. *What specific achievement should I shout more proudly about?* Well, I did a very difficult thing and left my full-time job to focus on my business, freelance writing work, and career as an author. It's been hugely scary, but I've managed to spend a full year getting myself paid for my creative work. That's incredible. *What is an affirmation I can use when I'm not feeling my own light?* I might jot down that I hope the affirmation card I draw will support me: I really struggle with feeling like I deserve a break, so I'm hoping to draw a card to warmly remind me that I've earned some rest.

Once I've journaled, I draw my cards. Here's what I've got:

Five of Pentacles   Four of Wands   Page of Wands

Before diving into each card individually, the first thing I do is take in the spread as a whole, paying attention to what stands out to me. Here are some of the things I notice:

There's a narrative through the weather and seasons. The cards from left to right move from winter to spring to summer.

The first two cards feature two figures, and the final card features only one.

There's one Pentacle card at the start, and two Wands follow it.

Sometimes these notes come to nothing, but other times they can be hugely helpful in understanding the spread. (Pay special attention, for instance, if two court cards are facing each other or facing away from each other—this tells you a lot about where you might be experiencing tension or alignment.)

Next, I try to give voice to the overall vibe I get from the spread and how that relates to the subject I'm addressing with the cards. The feeling I get looking at these cards, considering the shifting tone from Five of Pentacles to Four of Wands to Page of Wands, is that I'm getting where I need to go, but I need to recognize and celebrate the progress I've already made. In the context of the Sun Spread, it reminds me to trust that no matter what season I'm in, my creative sun is still rising every day. I can see a clear thread of advice telling me to take time to be proud of the hard work I do and to lavish my own achievements with the attention they deserve.

Now let's get into what the individual cards have to say to me:

I've drawn the Five of Pentacles to indicate where I need to give myself more credit, and it feels apt. This card speaks to me about how the last few months in my creative life have felt hard, cold, and like an endless slog. I'm working and working and working, but I'm not seeing the return yet, and I'm teetering on the edge of throwing in the towel. But this card also says, "Look how far you've made it, and you are SO CLOSE!" (Fun fact: I drew this spread just before turning in the manuscript for this book—I was, indeed, SO CLOSE!) The card helps me give myself credit for how far I've come, how much I've achieved, how hard it's been, and how close I've brought myself to the finish line. I pause and thank myself. Later this week, I might even tell my therapist for the first time in a long time that I'm proud of where I'm at.

I make note of how neatly this card tied into my pre-spread journaling. I DO need to give myself more credit for the resilience I've displayed in my creative life over the last few months. Even if I've felt left out in the cold, I've survived, and I've made progress, and it's time to tend to my tired mind, heart, and body. I deserve that.

Next, I've drawn the Four of Wands to symbolize a particular creative achievement I need to shout more about. I know immediately what this card's celebratory atmosphere is talking about: A few months ago (at the time of writing this), I published my first book. And while I did everything I could to market it, I didn't really take the time to celebrate the achievement in a human way. For the past couple of months, I've been toying with the idea of throwing a late dinner party for some friends—not as a work event, but as a private celebration of this very special moment in my creative life. This card affirms that hunch entirely. Shouting about an achievement doesn't have to mean SELLING; it can (and should!) also mean sharing from a place of love and warmth, and enjoying my own glow.

Finally, I've drawn the Page of Wands as an affirmation to help me feel the warmth of my own creative light. This is a card all about attentiveness, about looking so deeply into something that you can't help but feel

compelled by it. So, what I'm taking away from this card, and from the time spent doing this spread at all, is a reminder that the first step to feeling my light is to pay attention. If I look for my light, as I've done over the course of this spread, I'm guaranteed to see it, to feel it, and to be illuminated by it.

It's not the affirmation to rest that I'd hoped for (though notice that the Five of Pentacles covered that in its own way), but it's the battery charge I need for the moment.

I walk away from the spread feeling warm, basking in the glow of the impressive accomplishments the spread has invited me to reflect on, and with a few concrete actions: I'm going to give myself a little break after this wearying period. I'm going to invite friends and family over for drinks to celebrate my publication, and I'm going to be on the lookout every day for my own light; now that I know it's there, I'll give it the gift of my own attention.

Journaling with Tarot

I advise anyone who wants to build a more creative life using the tarot to start a tarot journal. That's why every card I discuss in this book comes with a journal prompt, alongside the other creative prompts.

When you record your responses to the cards as you work with them, you not only start to develop your own relationship to the cards, but you also start generating ideas in a low-pressure environment—ideas you can return to and spin into new creations anytime.

There is no right or wrong way to keep a tarot journal, and your approach will shift over time, depending on what you need. Over the following pages, you'll find some possible frameworks you can use to guide your tarot journaling practice.

Keep a Card-a-Day Journal

This one is easy; it just requires some consistency. All you need to do is draw one card every day—I often recommend first thing in the morning or before bed—and reflect on that card. You can use the journal prompts provided in this book, you can respond fully stream-of-conscious, or you can use the same prompts every day, regardless of the card you pull. If you go that final route, the following are some questions I like to use for my daily pulls:

What does this card remind me of in my life right now?

What action does this card inspire me to take?

What does this card inspire me to let go of?

What's the biggest lesson I can learn from this card?

Work with a Daily or Weekly Spread

If you like the idea of daily tarot journaling but need a little more stimulation than just one card a day, or if you want to practice storytelling through tarot, you might prefer to pull a regular spread instead of a daily card. Here is an easy spread I like to use. Simply pull cards for the same spread every day/each week (as you prefer) and journal about what each card brings up for you.

·❋ 1 ❋·

What energy can I step into today/this week?

·❋ 2 ❋·

What energy can I step away from today/this week?

·❋ 3 ❋·

How can I honor my creativity today/this week?

Work with One Card for a Week, Month, Season, or Year

If you're interested in doing a deeper dive and working with one card for a longer period of time, consider drawing or intentionally choosing a card to focus on for a specific length of time—anything between a week and a year. I'd still recommend daily journaling in which you explore the card and what it means to you each day, but you can do weekly journaling sessions instead if that's more sustainable for you.

You might want to set up a framework of questions to reflect on, like the following:

> How do I want to embody this card's energy in my life today/this week?
>
> What creative ideas is this card bringing up for me today/this week?
>
> What have I learned about this card since yesterday/last week?

Create a Tarot Ephemera Journal

I have lots of clients who like to get crafty with their journals instead of simply writing. I admire their creativity so much, and I often suggest that reticent journalers develop an ephemera or collage journaling habit rather than focusing on writing. Keep a stack of magazines, scrapbook paper, photos, or other paper goods on hand, as well as lots of glue and tape.

Then, choose one of the preceding formats (daily card, daily or weekly spread, long-term card focus) and create a collage in response to the cards you pull. It's an incredibly satisfying way to get creative and to nurture a low-pressure journaling habit.

Start a Tarot Blog

Nobody said you had to keep your tarot thoughts to yourself! If I hadn't started up Pip Cards Tarot in 2020 as a tarot blog on Instagram, you wouldn't be holding this book in your hands now.

So, if your creativity thrives on community and visibility, get yourself a tarot-focused blog, social media account, or newsletter, and start writing, vlogging, or podcasting your tarot journey. Give other tarot lovers the chance to connect with you and find new inroads with the cards through your unique point of view.

Tarot Spreads for Creativity

The following pages include seven spreads for creativity that I regularly use with my tarot clients and for myself. Like all the resources in this book, these spreads are designed to help you generate ideas, connect more deeply to your creativity, and unlock creative blocks. Feel free to adapt them for your own use, and if you want to share your readings using these spreads online, I'd love to see them! Tag me on Instagram (@pipcardstarot).

The He(art) of the Matter Spread

This sweet and helpful spread is designed to let loose your creative expression.

YOU CAN USE THIS SPREAD TO

Get started when you don't know how to begin

Work through moments of creative block

Clarify the message you're trying to convey through a creative project

Generate new ideas for content that speaks honestly to your audience

Frame difficult conversations with creative collaborators and team members

··✳ 2 ✳··

Why do I need to express it?

··✳ 3 ✳··

What am I bringing of myself to the work?

··✳ 1 ✳··

What needs to be expressed?

··✳ 5 ✳··

How do I begin?

··✳ 4 ✳··

What does the work mean to me?

HOW TO USE THIS SPREAD

Before you shuffle your deck, set an intention by lighting a candle or by putting on a song that matches the feeling you want to express creatively. Then, shuffle your deck until you're ready to stop, and draw five cards. Lay them out as shown in the pattern that follows and record your thoughts about how each card relates to the prompts in the spread.

The Unlock Your Block Spread

I love this spread for unlocking your block, and not just because it's shaped like a key. This spread is intended to help you have a frank and honest conversation with yourself about all the factors blocking your creativity. By understanding these, and giving yourself grace, you'll be able to unlock the door to a more satisfying creative experience.

HOW TO USE THIS SPREAD

This is one of those spreads where a healthy dose of pre-spread journaling can be hugely helpful. Before you shuffle, sit down with your notebook (or use a camera or voice recorder if you prefer) and reflect on what's bringing you to this spread now. What does your block feel like? How long have you been experiencing it? Why do you need to unblock now? Once you've explored these questions, shuffle your deck and draw seven cards, laying them out in the spread pattern that follows. Return to your journal and reflect on the insight and advice the cards have to offer.

YOU CAN USE THIS SPREAD TO

Unblock on a specific project

Reconnect to your creativity if things have been feeling generally stagnant

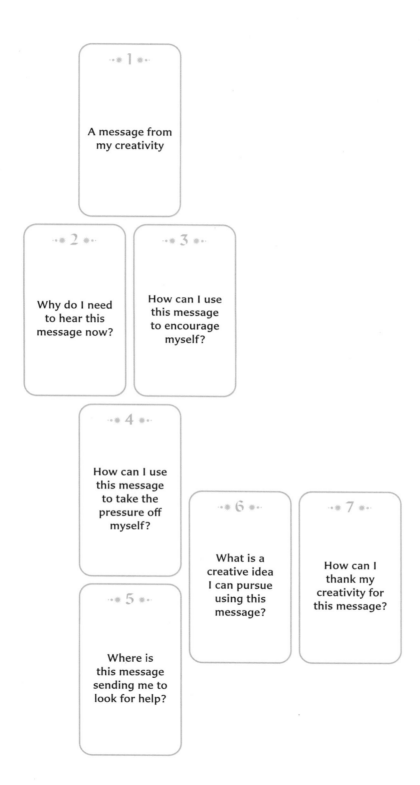

·•❋ 1 ❋•·

A message from
my creativity

·•❋ 2 ❋•·

Why do I need
to hear this
message now?

·•❋ 3 ❋•·

How can I use
this message
to encourage
myself?

·•❋ 4 ❋•·

How can I use
this message
to take the
pressure off
myself?

·•❋ 5 ❋•·

Where is
this message
sending me to
look for help?

·•❋ 6 ❋•·

What is a
creative idea
I can pursue
using this
message?

·•❋ 7 ❋•·

How can I
thank my
creativity for
this message?

The Muse Spread

There are many spreads within this book designed to help you connect to individual cards, but the Muse Spread is the mother of them all. This spread will help you find and connect with a card that can guide you on your creative journey—a card that can be your muse.

YOU CAN USE THIS SPREAD TO

Set intentions at the beginning of a project

Compose annual creative resolutions

Reset and get support when you're feeling uninspired

HOW TO USE THIS SPREAD

When pulling cards for the Muse Spread, you have two options: You can intentionally choose a card for the muse position that represents an energy you actively want to work with, or you can shuffle, draw a card at random, and let the deck decide your muse for you. Do whatever feels right. Once you've drawn or chosen your muse, sit with that card for a minute or two, just observing it and tapping into its energy. Then shuffle your deck and draw cards for the remaining five spread positions. Lay them out in the pattern that follows, and record your thoughts about how each card responds to the prompts in the spread.

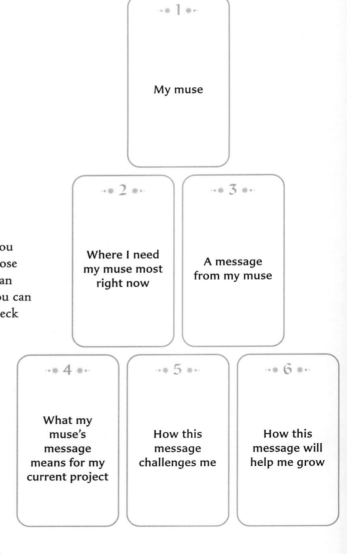

··*· 1 ·*··

My muse

··*· 2 ·*··

Where I need my muse most right now

··*· 3 ·*··

A message from my muse

··*· 4 ·*··

What my muse's message means for my current project

··*· 5 ·*··

How this message challenges me

··*· 6 ·*··

How this message will help me grow

The Fill My Cup Spread

Turn to this spread whenever you're feeling low on creative energy or in need of some creative self-care. The card pulls are designed to reconnect you to your creativity and to make your creative self feel seen, heard, and valued.

YOU CAN USE THIS SPREAD TO

Look after yourself and your creativity when you're burned out

Reconnect to your creativity after periods of stress

Bring play and kindness back to the forefront of your creative experience

HOW TO USE THIS SPREAD

Shuffle your cards and hold your deck to your heart. Take three deep breaths and invite your creativity to speak to you through the cards. Draw four cards, then lay them out as shown. Record your thoughts about how each card responds the prompts in the spread.

··❋ 1 ❋··

Where is my creativity asking for my attention?

··❋ 2 ❋··

What gift can I offer my creativity?

3

What's holding me back from giving this gift and my attention to my creativity?

··❋ 4 ❋··

How can I empower myself to give gifts and attention to my creativity?

The Story Builder Spread

The Story Builder is my absolute favorite spread to give to writers, but it's also useful for marketers and business owners who want to design more meaningful customer journeys. It's designed to help you plot out an entire story from start to finish, using tarot cards to identify the who, what, why, and how that will drive your story forward. The "what" row will help you figure out the main components of your plot, your characters, and what they are up against over the course of the story; the "why" row will help you figure out the underlying motivation and growth your main character experiences over the course of the story; and the "how" row will help you plot some specific events to help shape the beginning, middle, and end of the story.

HOW TO USE THIS SPREAD

I fully encourage you to get creative with this spread. You can of course shuffle and draw cards at random to generate a story idea. You can also use it as a storyboard and intentionally select cards to fit into the structure the spread provides—this may be a particularly helpful approach if you've already got a narrative or character in mind but need some help mapping out the big picture. And you can absolutely mix and match these tactics. I also like to use this spread to make a study of my favorite stories. When I read a particularly good book or watch a really compelling film, I use the tarot to map the story out against this spread, so I can see the mechanisms of how it came together and learn something as a writer.

YOU CAN USE THIS SPREAD TO

Generate ideas for a new story told through any medium

Troubleshoot areas of a current project

Reflect on what's working in your current project

Reflect on story structure in your favorite films, books, and the like

Design the customer journey you want to provide (imagine your customer as the main character of the story you're building)

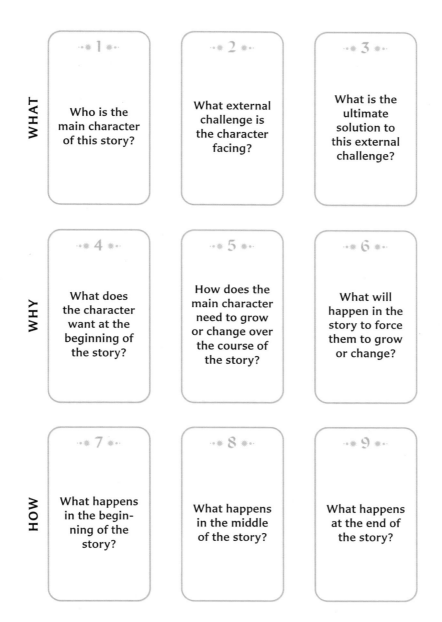

WHAT

·∗ 1 ∗·

Who is the main character of this story?

·∗ 2 ∗·

What external challenge is the character facing?

·∗ 3 ∗·

What is the ultimate solution to this external challenge?

WHY

·∗ 4 ∗·

What does the character want at the beginning of the story?

·∗ 5 ∗·

How does the main character need to grow or change over the course of the story?

·∗ 6 ∗·

What will happen in the story to force them to grow or change?

HOW

·∗ 7 ∗·

What happens in the beginning of the story?

·∗ 8 ∗·

What happens in the middle of the story?

·∗ 9 ∗·

What happens at the end of the story?

The Creative Business Spread

This is my go-to spread when working with creative business owners and entrepreneurs. It's great for helping you integrate your creative and strategic sides, so that you can show up creatively to your business. It makes for a great monthly check-in as part of your wider business strategy.

YOU CAN USE THIS SPREAD TO

Harness your creative expression for your business

Get more creative about solving problems in your business

Communicate to your customers

HOW TO USE THIS SPREAD

Shuffle your deck, then flip through until you find the Nine of Pentacles (the patron card of independent business owners) and split the deck into two stacks from there, shuffling the Nine of Pentacles back into either stack. Draw five cards from the larger stack and lay them out in the spread pattern that follows. Take notes on what the cards tell you, and keep the notes on file so you can refer back to them as part of your regular business check-ins.

·*· 4 ·*·

How do my expression, motivation, and experience serve my audience/customers?

·*· 3 ·*·

How can my experience so far help move my business forward?

·*· 1 ·*·

What do I want to express through my business?

·*· 5 ·*·

How can I innovate in alignment with my goals and unique business offerings?

·*· 2 ·*·

What motivates me as a business owner?

The Celtic Cross

The ten-card Celtic Cross is a traditional favorite for many tarot readers. I didn't invent it, but the version you're seeing here is my own adaptation of the classic spread. Each of the ten card positions is designed to give you specific insight into different aspects of a problem you're trying to solve, a question you're trying to answer, or a moment on your creative journey that you're trying to make sense of.

YOU CAN USE THIS SPREAD TO

Ask the cards a question about your creative journey

Explore a character in a story, book, or film (read as if you are the character drawing cards)

Understand your target audience/customer (read as if you are your ideal customer drawing cards)

(Note: I don't recommend reading tarot for any specific, real person who is not present or consenting, but it's totally ethical to use spreads to understand your theoretical "ideal" customer or audience.)

Because the Celtic Cross is a meaty spread with lots of scope, it works best when you ask a specific question before you start to draw cards, such as: Should I pursue project X or project Y? How can I grow as an artist? Am I ready to go back to school? What direction do I want to take my business in? Why am I blocked right now?

HOW TO USE THIS SPREAD

Shuffle your deck until you're ready to stop. Then, split the deck in half and set the two stacks side by side. Draw six cards from the deck on your right and lay them out in positions 1–6. Then draw four cards from the deck on your left and lay them out in positions 7–10. Take your time to reflect on what each card tells you and how they come together as a whole to offer insight into your question. You may want to take notes, and you may want to take a photo so you can come back to the cards later.

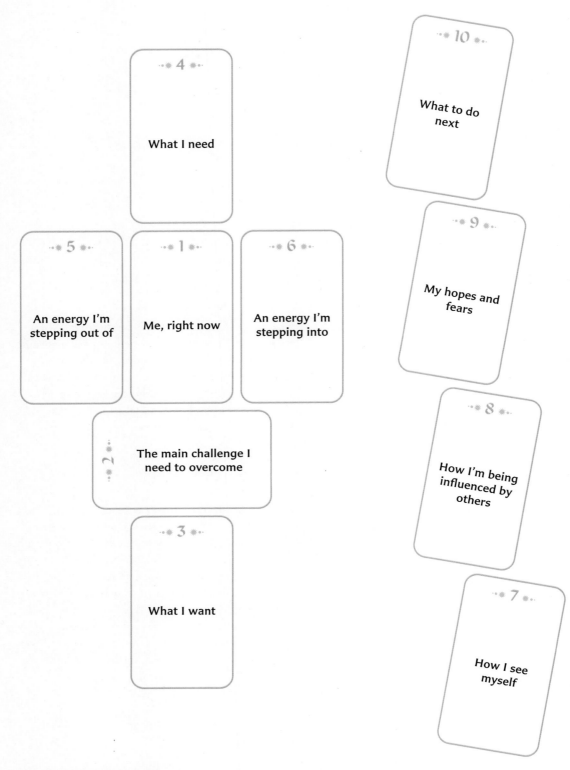

4

What I need

10

What to do
next

5

An energy I'm
stepping out of

1

Me, right now

6

An energy I'm
stepping into

9

My hopes and
fears

2

The main challenge I
need to overcome

8

How I'm being
influenced by
others

3

What I want

7

How I see
myself

Acknowledgments

This book would not be possible without the supportive shoulders of so many people (and several animals).

Thank you to my agent, Jane Graham Maw, for your patience, kindness, and expertise. Thanks to the wider GMC team—I'm honored to call myself one of yours. And thanks to Maddy Belton for your crucial early contributions to bringing this book into the world.

Thank you to the entire team at Chronicle, especially my editors Caitlin Kirkpatrick and Natalie Butterfield, for holding my hand to the end.

Thank you to my creative support system: my writing sisters, Katherine Dunn and Sara Gray—you are my role models; the London Writers Salon—this book would not exist without you and I would be a mess (Lindsey and Lauren, your support and kindness since the very beginning means more to me than I can ever say); Jen for reading the earliest version of what eventually became this book; Erica, Cloe, and Brady for getting me through the hard months in Boston when I began this book; Cara Hudson—I missed working with you on this one!; Ruth and Salomée at the Feminist Bookshop in Brighton; fellow tarot readers who inspire me, especially Nix Palomba, Claire Laizans, and Morgan Thomas; my therapist Maria; my tarot and creativity coaching clients—you make my dreams come true; all of my friends in London, Brighton, Avignon, and beyond; and my family: the Pippins, the Mizzis, and the Crabtrees.

Thank you to anyone who has shared, recommended, or otherwise supported my tarot work. You help me believe in myself, and that's a precious resource for a writer.

Books take a long time to make their way into the world; there are inevitably many people I've grown close to after finalizing this manuscript . . . please know how much I appreciate you.

Finally, thank you to Zacharie Mizzi, for all of it. I love you. And to my gorgeous babies, Fletcher and Figg: No one makes for better company while I write.

About the Author

Chelsey Pippin Mizzi is an American tarot reader and writer based in Avignon, France. She is the founder of Pip Cards Tarot, a tarot consultancy that helps creatives harness the power of tarot to beat block and burnout, generate ideas, and nurture their art practice. In addition to her published books (*Tarot for Creativity*, *The Tarot Spreads Yearbook*), her essays, journalism, and fiction have also been featured in BuzzFeed, Metro, *New York Magazine*, Creative Boom, HorrorTree, and Five Minute Lit.

For more from Chelsey, follow her on Instagram @pipcardstarot, or subscribe to her Substack, The Shuffle (theshuffle.substack.com), for fortnightly musings at the intersection of creativity and modern spirituality.

About the Artwork

The *Modern Way Tarot* puts a twenty-first-century spin on Pamela Colman Smith's classic tarot card designs. It retains the original symbolism but increases the emphasis on important visual elements, making it extremely easy to use for beginners and experts alike. To learn more about the project or to purchase the *Modern Way Tarot* deck and guidebook, please visit modernwaytarot.com.